BASQUE WOMEN'S EDUCATION
IN THE
18TH CENTURY
AN ATLANTIC ISSUE

DIASPORA AND MIGRATION STUDIES SERIES #17

BASQUE WOMEN'S EDUCATION IN THE 18TH CENTURY
AN ATLANTIC ISSUE

Iker Echeberria Ayllón

CENTER FOR BASQUE STUDIES
UNIVERSITY OF NEVADA, RENO
2023

This book was published with generous financial support from the Basque Government.

Center for Basque Studies
University of Nevada, Reno
1664 North Virginia St,
Reno, Nevada 89557 usa
http://basque.unr.edu

Copyright © 2023 by the Center for Basque Studies and the University of Nevada, Reno
ISBN-13: 978-1-949805-81-9
EPUB ISBN: 978-1-949805-82-6
All rights reserved.

Library of Congress Cataloging-in-Publication Data

Names: Echeberria Ayllón, Iker, author.
Title: Basque women's education in the 18th century : an Atlantic issue / Dr. Iker Echeberria Ayllón, Universidad del País Vasco/Euskal Herriko Unibertsitatea.
Description: Reno, Nevada : Center for Basque Studies, University of Nevada-Reno, [2023] | Includes bibliographical references. | Summary: "The volume provides an in-depth reflection on the ideology, practices and consequences of the implementation of systems of education directed to women during the 18th century within the broader space of the Basque community and from a diasporic perspective"-- Provided by publisher.
Identifiers: LCCN 2023022469 (print) | LCCN 2023022470 (ebook) | ISBN 9781949805819 (paperback) | ISBN 9781949805819 (epub)
Subjects: LCSH: Women, Basque--Education--Mexico--History. | Atlantic Ocean Region--Emigration and immigration. | Atlantic Ocean Region--History.
Classification: LCC LE8.M614 .E44 2023 (print) | LCC LE8.M614 (ebook) | DDC 370.899/920163--dc23/eng/20230606
LC record available at https://lccn.loc.gov/2023022469
LC ebook record available at https://lccn.loc.gov/2023022470

Printed in the United States of America

Contents

INTRODUCTION I

PART I: VIZCAYAN GIRLS IN MEXICO TO ATTEND SCHOOL 8

PART II: THE EDUCATION OF (SOME) BASQUE GIRLS DURING THE 18TH CENTURY 39

CONCLUSIONS 71

APPENDIX 84

BIBLIOGRAPHY 95

INDEX 111

INTRODUCTION

This study aims to analyze the education of Basque women during the eighteenth century.[1] However, before starting, there are a couple of issues I would like to address. First, this piece of research analyzes the changes that occurred in relation to the elite or most privileged groups. During the era in question, people, and most particularly young girls, rarely received a formal education, a circumstance that leads to a clear methodological problem due to the lack of documentary sources.

Given this difficulty, the present study aims to reflect the various historiographic efforts made to date in both the Basque Country and America. From the 1990s onward, many specialists on both sides of the Atlantic Ocean have been working in this field, although never before have their efforts been brought together. Moreover, the present study contains a series of novel documentary findings that help offer a clearer picture of the issue within a joint framework of reference.

Second, I would like to say a few words about the spatial framework of the study. The provinces of Guipúzcoa, Álava, Lordship of Vizcaya, and the Kingdom of Navarra were located in the north of the Iberian Peninsula on the border with France. Although politically they formed part of the Kingdom of Spain, during the period under study here, these regions had their own legal frameworks within this compound kingdom.[2] This is important to bear in mind, since the dynamics observed will help us understand the events that transpired from a broader perspective that extends beyond each individual province or even the Basque community itself. Furthermore, the problems outlined should be interpreted from a chronological and territorial perspective. Consequently, the analysis will reveal a series of relationships, interactions, and processes that unfold within a vast global, cisatlantic or transnational tableau.[3]

The history of Basque emigration to America and the role it played in the Kingdom of Spain's colonial expansion is written in letters of gold, or rather silver—or perhaps in letters of blood, depending on your point of view. It is a story that began with Elcano (the first person to circumnavigate the globe), Urdaneta, and their ancestors who were instrumental in opening up the West Indies Route (the system that connected the metropolis with America[4]), and ended in an interesting achievement: the so-called *Basque lobby*.[5]

Around 1668, the serious conflict that had hitherto disrupted Peru finally came to an end. It was a fight for control over the silver mines that had its roots in the war fought many years previously between the Basques and the Vicuñas (inhabitants of Castile and Andalusia) from the Iberian Peninsula.[6] Since 1625, the Basque colony in Alto Peru had managed to gain control over the quicksilver (and hence the silver) trade, its prominence in the economy and society of the viceroyalty had gone from strength to strength, a circumstance observed also in relation to Mexico.

The triumph of the north was, in reality, just one more chapter in the blood-soaked struggle for control of the silver trade that raged for centuries throughout the entire length of the Andes, giving rise to years of exploitation and domination. Meanwhile, the community of Basque emigrants grew steadily stronger from multiple different perspectives. In addition to their continuous victories in the interminable war to control the metal trade, they also enjoyed privileged access to and consideration by the Seville Consulate, the Court in Madrid and the Seville *Casa de Contratación*, all institutions responsible for managing the American monopoly.[7] Their position was so strong that, from the mid-seventeenth century onward, the northern influence in the West Indies Route was unmistakable, leading to the community of Basque emigrants often being considered a lobby. The sway of the Basque community (one of the most important communities of that period) was rooted in a number of different factors, including the specific social and economic characteristics of their place of origin, the relative stability of the migratory chains deployed, their unique language, unparalleled maritime and trade traditions and the support they received from institutions on the other side of the Atlantic.[8]

As a result of the asset concentration policy that was so common in the north of the Iberian Peninsula[9] and was also known as the single heir or primogeniture system, many second sons who were excluded from their family inheritance decided to leave home and seek their fortune elsewhere.[10] During the modern era, stories of wealth and honor from the New World were music to the ears of young men anxious to make their way in the world,[11] turning the system itself into a seedbed for emigration.[12] In light of this situation, the establishment of stable, reliable migratory chains became indispensable, resulting in the use by emigrants of preexisting social bonds and relationships, without the need to generate new and specific instruments for this purpose.[13] Within this ordered and structured migratory chain, the uncle-nephew relationship proved of the utmost importance,[14] as did the goodwill of a local patron and the support of fellow countrymen.

The age-old Basque tradition and knowhow in strategic sectors such as seafaring, shipbuilding, and trade, which had flourished from at least medieval times onward,[15] were important aspects that help explain the more or less regular flow of human migrants to America. The strong presence of the Basque community since the Conquest, coupled with the development during this period of the *foral* system of rights and privileges, partly explains this successful mobility, since any attempt to understand the extraordinary influence exercised by the Basque colony throughout the vast Spanish colonial empire must necessarily take into account its maritime culture.[16] The Lordship of Vizcaya and the provinces of Álava and Guipúzcoa were regions closely linked to the sea and to the economic activities derived from it, sectors which proved very lucrative within the context of a customs regime that turned borderlands into free trade zones.

These *foral* regimes, and in particular those in effect in Guipúzcoa and Vizcaya, were based on a plethora of different arguments,[17] although perhaps the most weighty one was linked to the nobility of their inhabitants, which translated into universal nobility. The cornerstone of the system was the fact that these rights and privileges had been attained by Vizcaya in the *Fuero Nuevo* of 1526.[18] The inhabitants of Guipúzcoa, on the other hand, had to wait until 1638 before being similarly compensated for having successfully defended the border with France.[19] Basque emigrants therefore had a strategic advantage: the privileged status of nobility.[20]

This community had a penchant for creating powerful lobbies within devotional foundations, political institutions and companies. As links in the solid Basque chain covering the West Indies Route, those who emigrated during the second half of the seventeenth century could count on the support of fellow countrymen who were well-established within the Seville trade hub, the Royal Court and the System of Fleets and Galleons.[21] To this we must add the pressure exerted by the Guipúzcoa and Vizcaya Provincial Parliaments (*Juntas Generales*) and expat organizations throughout the length and breadth of the vast Spanish Empire. These organizations, dedicated to a patron saint, brought Basques together and served as spaces for lobbying and community-building.[22]

From here on, one of the most interesting questions we should be asking ourselves is how to understand the true impact of the flow of money from America to the north of the Iberian Peninsula, remittances that were linked to the Atlantic circuit and which helped mitigate the effects of what has become known as the Crisis of 1600, which continued throughout the entire Modern Age.[23] Since this is an unquantifiable phenomenon, our knowledge of it mainly consists of estimations, such as the figures recorded by a scribe from Seville who, over the course of eighteen years between 1630 and 1690, sent approximately thirty-two million *reales de vellón* to San Sebastián. However, the most impressive figure reported by one of the most comprehensive studies carried out to date estimates that, during the second half of the seventeenth century, 23% of all private remittances sent to Seville from America ended up directly in the Basque provinces.[24] Despite the lack of real facts and figures, these statistics indicate a business of immense proportions.

These were the foundations of the power and influence exercised by the Basque territories within the Spanish Empire, particularly in America. As a phenomenon or process linked to and benefiting from this context, women's education cannot be understood without taking these circumstances into account.

The main objective of this paper is, therefore, to analyze the education of Basque women within this Atlantic context. There is a whole diversity of proposals, projects and educational canons historically connected to each other, approaches that help to understand the historical evolution of Basque femininity throughout the eighteenth century.

One of the main contributions of the book is to relate the different episodes lived, events analyzed in an atomized way. A good part of the different historical events that comprise this story have been studied previously, although partially and locally. That is why this research will help connect some unconnected realities to date. The history of Basque female formation throughout the seventeenth century, I maintain, involves a whole series of communities perfectly settled in different points of the Hispanic Monarchy, a universe connected by capital, interests, disputes, values or ideas.

Through the different educational models proposed in the seventeenth century, both in the Basque Country and America, we will also observe the changes: from a growing concern for the formation of the smallest, to the new model of eighteenth-century femininity, passing through interactions and disputes carried out by the different historical agents. A whole series of characters and institutions will dominate the scene trying to impose their criteria. Since then, concepts such as femininity itself or the formation of girls will be forever transformed.

Notes

1   This work brings together and expands part of my doctoral thesis. Likewise, its elaboration has been possible thanks to the Postdoctoral Program for the Improvement of Doctoral Research Staff financed by the Basque Government and under the auspices of the *Society, Power and Culture Research Group (XIV-XVIII centuries)*, of the University of the Basque

Country/Euskal Herriko Unibertsitatea and in collaboration with the Center for Basque Studies , the University of Nevada, Reno.

2   Although historiographically inaccurate, from now on I will also refer to these territories as the Basque Country, including the Kingdom of Navarre. I point out the same about the viceroyalty of New Spain, which I will refer to as Mexico.

3   David Armitage, "Tres conceptos de historia atlántica," *Revista de Occidente* 281 (2004): 20.

4   Álvaro Aragón Ruano, "La evolución de la economía guipuzcoana en tiempos de Urdaneta: un período de desarrollo y expansión entre supuestas crisis," in *Andrés de Urdaneta: un hombre moderno*, ed. Susana Truchuelo García (Ordizia: Ordiziako Udala, 2009), 119-144; José Antonio Azpiazu Elorza, "Los guipuzcoanos y Sevilla en la Alta Edad Moderna," *Itsas Memoria. Revista de Estudios Marítimos del País Vasco* 4 (2003): 207-213; Lutgardo García Fuentes, "Los vascos en la Carrera de Indias en la Edad Moderna: una minoría dominante," *Temas Americanistas* 16 (2003): 33-40.

5   Alberto Angulo Morales, "Los hidalgos norteños en el centro de un Imperio: Madrid (1638-1850). Negocios, política e identidad" en *Recuperando el Norte: empresas, capitales y proyectos atlánticos en la economía imperial hispánica*, ed. Alberto Angulo Morales and Álvaro Aragón Ruano (Bilbao: UPV/EHU, 2016) 261-296; Alfonso de Otazu and José Ramón Díaz de Durana, *El espíritu emprendedor de los vascos* (Madrid: Sílex, 2008), 246-258; Tamar Herzog, "Private Organizations as Global Networks in Early Modern Spain and Spanish America," in *The Collective and the Public in Latin America: Cultural Identities and Political Order*, ed. Luis Roniger and Tamar Herzog (Brighton: Sussex Academic Press, 2000), 117-133.

6   Alberto Angulo Morales, "El *institutional entangled global network* de navarros y vascongados en la defensa atlántica por la plata peruana del Seiscientos (Madrid, Potosí y Puno)," *Protohistoria* 35 (2021): 361-378; Bernd Hausberger, "La guerra de los vicuñas contra los vascongados en Potosí y la etnización de los vascos a principios de la Edad Moderna," in *Excluir para ser. Procesos identitarios y fronteras sociales en la América hispánica (siglos XVII-XVIII)*, ed. Christian Büschges and Frédérique Langue (Madrid: Iberoamericana, 2005), 23-58; Jurgi Kintana Goirienea, "La "nación vascongada" y sus luchas en el Potosí del siglo XVII. Fuentes de estudio y estado de la cuestión," *Anuario de Estudios Americanos* 59-1 (2002): 287-310; Otazu and Díaz de Durana, *El espíritu emprendedor de los vascos*, 332-347.

7   Fernando Fernández González, "Castilla, Sevilla y el País Vasco en la segunda mitad del siglo XVIII," *Itsas Memoria. Revista de Estudios Marítimos del País Vasco* 4 (2003): 287-295.

8   For an introduction to the Atlantic World, John H. Elliott, *Imperios del mundo atlántico. España y Gran Bretaña en América, 1492-1830* (Madrid: Taurus, 2006); John H. Elliott, *España, Europa y el mundo de ultramar (1500-1800)* (Madrid: Taurus, 2010).

9   Daniel Baldellou Monclús, "Idiosincrasia del modelo de transmisión de la propiedad en el Antiguo Régimen: el modelo de las familias del Pirineo," *Actas del I Congreso Internacional Jóvenes Investigadores Siglo de Oro*, (2012): 11-21; Daniel Baldellou Monclús and José Antonio Salas Ausens, "Noviazgo y matrimonio en Aragón. Casarse en la Europa del Antiguo Régimen," *Revista de Historia Moderna. Anales de la Universidad de Alicante* 34 (2016): 85; Pilar Erdozain Azpilikueta, and Fernando Mikelarena Peña, "Algunas consideraciones en torno a la investigación del régimen de herencia troncal en la Euskal Herria tradicional," *Vasconia* 28 (1991): 71-91; José Antonio Moreno Almárcegui and Ana Zabalza Seguín, *El origen histórico de un sistema de heredero único. El prepirineo navarro, 1540-1739* (Pamplona: Rialp, 1999); Ana Zabalza Seguín, "El heredero ideal: prácticas

sucesorias en la Navarra pirenaica durante la Edad Moderna (1550-1725)," in *Actas del Congreso Internacional de la Población: V Congreso de la ADEH*, ed. David Sven Reher Sullivan (Logroño: 1999): 239-250.

10   Alberto Angulo Morales, De Cameros a Bilbao. Negocios, familia y nobleza en tiempos de crisis (1770-1834) (Bilbao: UPV/EHU, 2007), 89-95; Juan Aranzadi, Milenarismo vasco. Edad de Oro, etnia y nativismo (Madrid: Taurus, 2000), 535-545; Jesús Arpal Poblador, La sociedad tradicional en el País Vasco: el estamento de los hidalgos en Guipúzcoa (San Sebastián: Haranburu, 1979), 213-243; José María Imízcoz Beunza (Ed.), Casa, familia y sociedad (País Vasco, España y América, siglos XV-XIX) (Leioa: UPV/EHU, 2004).

11   Johnni Langer, "O mito do Eldorado: origem e significado no imaginário sul-americano (século XVI)," *Revista de História* 136 (1997): 26-28.

12   Óscar Álvarez Gila and Alberto Angulo Morales, *Las migraciones vascas en perspectiva histórica (siglos XVI-XX)* (Bilbao: UPV/EHU, 2002); Alberto Angulo Morales and Álvaro Aragón Ruano (Ed.), *Recuperando el Norte. Empresas, capitales y proyectos atlánticos en la economía imperial hispánica* (Bilbao: UPV/EHU, 2016); Alberto Angulo Morales, "Los frutos de la movilidad. La emigración norteña peninsular en Madrid y el Imperio (siglos XVII y XVIII)," *Obradoiro de Historia Moderna* 24 (2015): 113-139; Alberto Angulo Morales, "Migration, Mobility and Voyages. A Case Study on the Use of Private Sources for the Understanding of Basque Migration in the Eighteenth Century," in *From the Records of my Deepest Memory. Personal Sources and the Study of European Migration, eighteenth-20th centuries*, ed. Óscar Álvarez Gila and Alberto Angulo Morales (Bilbao: UPV/EHU, 2016), 13-40; José Miguel Aramburu-Zudaire, "América y los vascos en la Edad Moderna. Una perspectiva historiográfica," *Vasconia* 34 (2005): 249-274; José Manuel Azcona Pastor, *Identidad y estructura de la emigración vasca y navarra hacia Iberoamérica (siglos XVI-XXI)* (Madrid: Thomson Reuters-Aranzadi, 2015).

13   Álvarez Gila and Angulo Morales, Las migraciones vascas en perspectiva histórica (siglos XVI-XX), 94.

14   Ibid., 107-108.

15   José Ángel Lema Pueyo, "De "Ipuzkoa" a la hermandad de villas de Gipuzkoa (ss. VI-VX)," in *Síntesis de la Historia de Gipuzkoa*, ed. Álvaro Aragón Ruano and Iker Echeberria Ayllón (Donostia: Diputación Foral de Gipuzkoa, 2017), 208-210.

16   Aragón Ruano, Álvaro, "Euskal Herria «itsastarra» lehen mundubiraren testuinguruan," in *Elkano eta lehen mundubira: 500 urte geroago* (Getaria: Mundubira 500 Elkano Fundazioa, 2020), 75-102; Estíbaliz González Dios, "Gipuzkoa en la primera globalización (ss. XVI-XVIII)," in *Síntesis de la Historia de Gipuzkoa*, ed. Álvaro Aragón Ruano and Iker Echeberria Ayllón (Donostia: Diputación Foral de Gipuzkoa, 2017), 299-302.

17   Notitia Vasconiae. Historiadores, juristas y pensadores políticos de Vasconia. Antigüedad, Edad Media y Moderna (Madrid: Fundación Iura Vasconiae, Marcial Pons, 2019).

18   José Ramón Díaz de Durana, "La hidalguía universal en el País Vasco. Tópicos sobre sus orígenes y causas de su desigual generalización," *Cuadernos de Alzate* 31 (2004): 55-57.

19   Alberto Angulo Morales "Información, negociación y defensa. Las fronteras en las provincias exentas (XVI-XVII)," in *Dinámica de las fronteras en periodos de conflicto. El Imperio español (1640-1815)*, ed. Miguel Ángel Melón Jiménez, Miguel Rodríguez Cancho and Isabel Testón Núñez (Cáceres: Universidad de Extremadura, 2019), 154-167; Álvaro Aragón Ruano, ""...Faltar y ausentarse con esto los naturales de esta provinçia y quedar

despoblada y hierma, sin defensa alguna...." Discursos de frontera en Gipuzkoa durante la Edad Moderna," in *Naciones en el Estado-Nación: la formación cultural y política de naciones en la Europa contemporánea*, ed. Joseba Agirreazkuenaga Zigorraga, Joseba y Eduardo J. Alonso Olea (Barcelona: Editorial Base, 2014), 404-405; González Dios, "Gipuzkoa en la primera globalización (ss. XVI-XVIII)," 291-292.

20   On the importance of border discourses for forality, see Álvaro Aragón Ruano, "Discursos de frontera en el Pirineo occidental durante la Edad Moderna," in *Una década prodigiosa. Beligerancia y negociación entre la Corona y las provincias vascas (1717-1728)*, ed. Álvaro Aragón Ruano and Alberto Angulo Morales (Bilbao: UPV/EHU, 2019), 155-174.

21   Álvaro Aragón Ruano and Alberto Angulo Morales, "Spanish Basque Country in Global Trade Networks in the Eighteenth Century," *International Journal of Maritime History* 25-1 (2013): 149-172; Lutgardo García Fuentes, *Los peruleros y el comercio de Sevilla con las Indias, 1580-1630* (Sevilla: Universidad de Sevilla, 1997); Lutgardo García Fuentes, "Los vascos," 29-49; José Garmendia Arruebarrena, *Cádiz, los vascos y la carrera de Indias* (San Sebastián: Eusko Ikaskuntza, 1989); Jesús Turiso Sebastián, "Emigración, comerciantes y comercio en la región de Veracruz entre 1778-1822," *Naveg@mérica* 22 (2019): 11.

22   Alberto Angulo Morales, "Otro "imposible vencido": hombres, provincias y reinos en la Corte en tiempos de Carlos II," in *Volver a la «hora navarra». La contribución navarra a la construcción de la monarquía española en el siglo XVIII*, ed. Rafael Torres Sánchez (Pamplona: Universidad de Navarra, 2010), 33-72; Alberto Angulo Morales, "De la congregación de Cantabria o San Ignacio al proyecto de la Bascongada. El grupo de presión vasco en la Villa y Corte de Madrid (1713-1775)," in *Devoción, paisanaje e identidad. Las cofradías y congregaciones de naturales en España y en América (siglos XVI-XIX)*, ed. Óscar Álvarez Gila, Alberto Angulo Morales, Alberto and Jon Ander Ramos Martínez (Bilbao: UPV/EHU, 2014), 199-226; Alberto Angulo Morales and Álvaro Aragón Ruano, *Recuperando el Norte. Empresas, capitales y proyectos atlánticos en la economía imperial hispánica*.

23   Álvaro Aragón Ruano and Xabier Alberdi Lonbide, "El premio de la plata y la devaluación del vellón en Guipúzcoa en el siglo XVII," *Cuadernos de Historia Moderna* 27 (2002): 131-167; María Lourdes Odriozola Oyarbide and María Montserrat Gárate Ojanguren, "Emigración y remesas de capitales. Siglos XVIII-XIX," in *Los movimientos migratorios en la construcción de las sociedades modernas*, ed. Karmele Zarraga Sangroniz and Manuel González Portilla (Bilbao: UPV/EHU, 1996), 471-488; Juan Javier Pescador, *"The New World inside a Basque villaje: the Oiartzun Valley and its Atlantic exchanges, 1550-1800"* (PhD diss., University of Michigan, 1998); Juan Javier Pescador, *Familias y fortunas del Oiartzun antiguo. Microhistoria y genealogía, siglos XVI-XVIII* (Oiartzun: Oiartzungo Udala, 1995).

24   Fernando Fernández González, *Comerciantes vascos en Sevilla, 1650-1700* (Vitoria-Gasteiz: Diputación de Sevilla/Gobierno Vasco, 2000), 277-284. See also Alberto Angulo Morales, "Mercados y financieros vascos. El circuito de la plata y su control en el Seiscientos," in *Tesoreros, "arrendadores" y financieros en los reinos hispánicos. La Corona de Castilla y el Reino de Navarra (siglos XIV-XVII)*, ed. Ernesto García Fernández (Madrid: Ministerio de Economía y Hacienda, Instituto de Estudios Fiscales, 2012), 241-256; Lutgardo García Fuentes, "La crisis del siglo XVII y las remesas de caudales indianos desde Sevilla para el País Vasco," *Archivo hispalense. Revista histórica, literaria y artística* 84-255 (2001): 27-42; Jesús María Usunáriz Garayoa, "Un aspecto de la emigración navarra al Nuevo Mundo durante el siglo XVIII: las remesas indianas," *Príncipe de Viana* 13 (1991): 383-392.

PART I

VIZCAYAN GIRLS IN MEXICO TO ATTEND SCHOOL

THE FOUNDATIONS OF A LANDMARK MOMENT

According to the founding myth, it was a normal day at the beginning of the eighteenth century when an affluent general of Basque origin started to hand out pennies to several children in Mexico City. Suddenly, he noticed something startling: a young girl with blond hair stood out among the crowd, and when asked, admitted to being of Basque descent. At that very moment, the general decided to set up a school to ensure her education.[1]

To understand the origin of the *Real Colegio de San Ignacio de México* (Royal School of Saint Ignatius Mexico),[2] popularly known as the *Vizcaínas* School (or the Vizcayan Girls' School), we must return to the dynamics of Basque emigration to America.[3] As is so often the case in history, the roots of this landmark event are a combination of different dynamics, phenomena and multiple connected (or connectable) elements. We should not forget that historical processes are multifaceted in nature and full of sharp angles and edges.

Basques had been present on the new continent since the conquest of America, and over centuries of colonial rule and domination had become increasingly powerful. Taking advantage of their position at the head of the new system, many Basques gained privileged positions, gradually forming a dense network within the Spanish Empire known as the Basque lobby, which in turn served as a magnet for future countrymen. Thanks to this notable presence, which caused them to stand out from other communities of emigrants from the Iberian Peninsula, their role in future events of all kinds would be crucial, as would their intervention in the development of women's education throughout the early modern period.

At the beginning of the Empire's dominion over New Spain, the first bishop of the Mexican dioceses and the second in the history of the viceroyalty, the Basque cleric Juan de Zumárraga, supported the foundation of several different institutions, one of which was the *Colegio de la Madre de Dios* (the School of the Mother of God), established by the first mission of Spanish nuns sent to Mexico. The mission had a twofold purpose, to convert and to educate young females by setting up a network of schools for indigenous girls throughout Mexico, Texcoco, Tehuacán, Xochimilco, Cuautitlán, Otumba, Tlaxcala, Tepeapulco, Chalco, Huejotzingo, Cholula, and Coyoacán. The mission also founded the first convent in the history of America, the *Convento de la Concepción* (the Convent of the Conception).[4]

From that time onward, part of the New Spanish female population, specifically the creole community, would have the opportunity to attend a series of schools known as *Las Amigas* (The Friends). This small network of what could be considered public schools spread to wherever there was a large Hispanic community, although absenteeism was always high. Educated by poorly qualified teachers and always in dire need of money, girls learned the rudiments of reading, writing, domestic skills, and Catholic doctrine.[5] "After having gone to an '*Amiga*,' young women could only access books in their family home."[6]

Basque intervention in women's education did not start until the eighteenth century, when the community of emigrants was at its height. But the period of expansion that followed would forever transform the weak educational network that had existed until then.

Founded at the end of the seventeenth century, the *San Miguel and San Francisco Xavier* retreat (dedicated to Saint Michael and to Saint Francis Xavier, patron saint of Navarra) provided an education to young girls from the poorest creole and mestizo communities of the capital. Known among the local population as the Belem retreat, the institution welcomed all "spinsters, widows with daughters, fallen women and young girls on the verge of falling into sin."[7] Faithful to its model, the retreat adhered to a rigorous cloister regime that was in reality more like a prison, in which entry was voluntary but leaving was well-nigh impossible. Over the years, however, this establishment (which was dependent on the archbishopric) gradually changed from a strict retreat dedicated to Catholicism, prayer, and work, to a unique educational model.[8]

It was the Basque archbishop José de Lanciego y Eguilaz who was mainly responsible for (or witness to) this metamorphosis—another of his outstanding works will consist of transforming the Hospital de la Misericordia into a retreat for divorcees.[9] During his mandate from 1712 to 1728, the residents of the city started to call the retreat *Colegio de Belem* (Belem School). As a result of these changes and the fact that the school began to earn itself a good reputation as a place where girls were educated for either marriage or convent life, the institution began to arouse a certain degree of interest among families living in the capital, who began to send their daughters there.[10] Young girls were taught Christian doctrine, reading, writing, basic arithmetic and "the tasks appropriate to their sex," which mainly consisted of the "feminine arts" of the time, linked to sewing, flower arranging, and embroidery.[11] As the century wore on, music was also included and indeed soon became a field in which the institution excelled.

Girls' education was therefore oriented toward one of the two options open to the women of that era under Tridentine decrees: marriage or religious vows. There was a third option, becoming a spinster, but that was socially frowned upon.

Within the framework that interests us, i.e., that of the Spanish Empire, female education was strictly controlled and directed throughout the entire early modern period and depended on one's social status. Therefore, in addition to the clearly gender-based establishment of education and training, which was rooted in assumptions about how households were organized and how the entire social, patriarchal and androcentric structure operated, there was also a division in terms of educational content in accordance with the place girls were expected to occupy in the social hierarchy. Although all women were trained to perform specific tasks and duties within the family unit (with the house as their universe), socioeconomic differences established certain barriers between different groups.

From the end of the sixteenth century, and coinciding with the expansion of the Tridentine reform, the archetype of the perfect married women, as portrayed by Fray Luis de León, was that of a "good wife," an image that sank deep into the mindset of Hispanic culture during the following centuries.[12] Women were viewed as the guardians and overseers of family order, under the shadow of the paterfamilias. They conserved their sexual integrity as a second dowry deposited in the lineage[13] and were hailed as the defenders of a model and image that was indispensable for both family and community wellbeing. The Humanist movement, led by thinkers such as Erasmus of Rotterdam, Luther and Vives,[14] enlivened the debate, reformulating the hitherto dominant perception of women's education.[15] While still constraining them to the home, and without completely doing away with the traditional view of their inferior nature and intelligence, humanist contributions nevertheless called for more women's education. Consequently, three major developments converged in the middle of the seventeenth century: an increase in the number of schools, the establishment of the first curriculum and the rise of new approaches.[16]

These changes prompted the appearance of projects such as the *Compañía de María* (Company of Mary), the spread of which throughout the Spanish Empire, including New Spain, played a key role in the story we are concerned with here.

These new debates, which arose with unprecedented force in response to the French *Querelle des femmes*, reflected the struggle between those in favor of continuing to defend the idea of women as inferior and those who asserted their equal capacity. Sometime later, famous women such as Mme. de Lambert demanded equal access to culture in order to enable women's intellectual development, a process that would, hypothetically at least, put an end to the age-old division between the sexes. If man was known for his Reason, women were known for their Sensitivity, prejudices that only began to be broken down well into the eighteenth century.

Far from being the principal battleground of these discourses, the seventeenth century saw only the commencement of these rejoinders, and constituted a series of decades in which the unusual role played by some women (mainly from France) began to change the nature of the debate about women's education. This in turn gave rise to the emergence of one of the best-known European treatises on women's education of the modern age: Fénelon's *Education des filles*, a work that "exercises prudence, procuring an education that, far from permitting the *denaturalization* of women, protects the designs of Nature and Society. Educating women should mean, firstly, providing them with a *feminine* character and morality, characterized by contention and religious and family feelings [...] In general, it proposes reading, writing and home sciences";[17] in other words, the model endorsed by Belem School in Mexico City.

The reading material to which attendees at the school had access included the principal Hispanic treatises of the period, such as *Mística Ciudad de Dios* by María Jesús de Ágreda, *Doctrina Cristiana* by Cardinal Belarmino and *Lo temporal y Eterno* by the Hispanic Jesuit Eusebio de Nieremberg. This last author, for example, remained a prominent figure in New Spanish culture until well into the nineteenth century, since his works were sold at the time by a bookseller of Basque descent located in Mexico City, María Fernández de Jáuregui.[18]

The rejection of cultured women with extensive intellectual knowledge—those "precious women" who shone in the literary salons of Louis XIV's France enjoyed widespread social support, with much mockery and criticism being leveled at pedantic ladies who were dismissed as know-it-alls. Women's intellectual development[19] was ridiculed by both Molière, in his well-known work *Les Précieuses ridicules*,[20] and by Francisco de Quevedo in *La culta latiniparla*.[21]

Works such as Fénelon's therefore served to intensify a growing concern. Reading, writing, and the performance of the duties appropriate to the female sex (such as sewing, for instance) began to feature in the curriculums (if indeed they can be described as such) of institutions offering education to women; institutions which, incidentally, had begun to emerge from the advent of Humanism onward.

Arising as it did in this context, Belem School benefited during the first half of the eighteenth century from the support (or interference) of a series of people of Basque origin. Juan Antonio de Vizarrón y Eguiarreta, Archbishop of Mexico, born in Cádiz (Spain) and Viceroy between 1734 and 1740, would be the main driving force behind the establishment of the institution's Music School, thanks to which it reached new heights of popularity. From this period on, music became highly appreciated as an eminently feminine aptitude and sensibility and was a key part of the training provided to women. According to the precepts of the period, well-educated wives were expected to perform certain social functions as the person responsible for the good image of the family, shining in society in order to make their relatives proud. Referring to the women with a good knowledge of music who left the Belem school to get married, Josefina Muriel points out that the suitors valued them and required them for their knowledge and [musical] virtues 'even without a marriage dowry,' as Archbishop Rubio y Salinas informed the king shortly afterwards."[22]

Another archbishop, José de Gárate, established the first scholarships at Belem School for students of Basque origin. This was in the year 1729 and the powerful community of *vizcaínos* (the term used during that period to refer to the Basques) in Mexico City was on the verge of setting its famous project in motion. These scholarships, of which there were twenty-four in total, served as a starting point for everything that came afterwards—among other outstanding donations made by notables of Basque origin we find those of Francisco Fernández de Uribe, the census worth 12,750 pesos of the Marquis of San Miguel de Aguayo or the rustic properties offered by Archbishop Juan Antonio de Vizarrón y Eguiarreta.[23] In the meantime, in 1721, the doctor of Basque origin, Ignacio de Castorena y Ursúa, considered to be the father of Hispano-American journalism for having created the *Gaceta de México* (Mexican Gazette), founded the *Los mil ángeles custodios de María Santísima* girls' school. It was also during this period that one of the New Spanish figures that would later transform women's education set off on her long voyage.

María Ignacia de Azlor y Echeverz was born on October 9, 1715 in the old province of Nueva Vizcaya, Mexico.[24] Daughter of José de Azlor y Virto de Vera, governor of Texas from 1719 to 1722,[25] she belonged to the New Spanish elite and was a member of the family that held title to the marquisate of San Miguel de Aguayo. However, the most interesting thing about her family history is the fact that it represents to a tee the importance of Atlantic dynamics in the historical development of events occurring on both sides of the ocean.

Many years earlier, María Ignacia's mother, Ignacia Xaviera de Echeverz, accompanied her family when they moved to the Kingdom of Navarra. Born in Mexico, she would spend the next thirty years on the family's Navarran estates. There she would give birth to María Josefa de Azlor y Echeverz, the fruit of her third marriage to the aforementioned José de Alzor y Virto de Vera and future heiress to the family estate and title. However, after thirty years of living at a distance from their vast American possessions, the family decided they could no longer control them from afar and returned to Mexico. It was there that María de Ignacia de Alzor y Echeverz was born, the woman who would become the founder of the first Company of Mary convent in the history of America.[26]

A sister organization of the Society of Jesus, at the critical period of its expansion into New Spain, the Company of Mary had a good reputation as an order dedicated to educating women. The close ties cultivated between the two orders prompted Ignacia to identify them as one and the same, describing the Company of Mary as "in all ways similar to the Society of Jesus."[27] And she was not far off the mark, since the pedagogical principles of the Company of Mary were indeed inspired by the Jesuit order founded by the Basque priest Saint Ignatius of Loyola.[28] Ignatian spirituality had a strong influence on the establishment of the Company of Mary, and also served as a symbol of union between Basques resident throughout the vast Spanish Empire. As a symbol of identity, this common source of devotion served to forge close ties between all emigrants of Basque origin.

The Company of Mary established institutions governed by a prioress that housed a small community of nuns who also worked as teachers. The convents accepted both live-in and day students, the former residing in the same building as the nuns, although separate from them, and the latter attending classes on a daily basis in order to receive a free education from teachers and caregivers, as part of a public school system that, in the case of Mexico, was not established until some years later. The basics of the education received by these students was centered around Catholic doctrine, reading, writing, courteousness, devotion, and "all manner of domestic skills," which mainly consisted of manual and material tasks linked to general culture.[29] In this way, the work of Jeanne de Lestonnac spread throughout the Hispanic world in the form of free schooling for local girls of Spanish and creole origin, or at least for the most privileged ones from the high colonial classes.[30]

Given her mother's experience, it is hardly surprising that, during her childhood, María Ignacia heard tell of the convent that the Company of Mary had built in Tudela, Navarra, at the end of the seventeenth century. After receiving a meticulous education in the impressive library of her family home, in 1735, young María Ignacia decided to set out for the Tudela *Enseñanza*, the name given to the Company of Mary convents during that period.[31]

After a long journey and several years visiting her father's family in Zaragoza (Kingdom of Aragón, Spain), on September 24, 1742, María Ignacia de Alzor y Echeverz joined the Company of Mary, taking her vows in 1745. There, she occupied the position of sacristan, health prefect and teacher.[32]

Drawing on her sizable inheritance, in 1753 she decided to prepare to return to America with the firm intention of founding the first convent of the Company of Mary on that continent. It was a plan she had been developing since the moment she took her vows, reasoning that, since she had to renounce all her worldly goods, she may as well use them to the benefit of her Order. Given her social status, she received all manner of support. Indeed, in 1745, the same year in which she took her vows, she managed to persuade the king to approve her project by royal decree, and in 1752 she received a royal writ authorizing the foundation of her new convent. She immediately set sail for Mexico, accompanied by ten nuns from her Company, most of whom were Basque. The establishment of the convent in Mexico was also sponsored by the Society of Jesus, which: "fought to obtain the royal permits [...] the General of the Society charged Father Bernardo Pazuegos, S.J. with accompanying the nuns during their voyage. The monarchs, who also sympathized with the undertaking, did not just approve it; the queen donated 3,000 pesos to cover the costs of the journey, and the king sent a royal ship to accompany the voyagers as far as the Canary Islands."[33]

Welcomed with much fanfare upon their arrival in Mexico in 1753, the group of nuns did not take long to establish the *Nuestra Señora del Pilar* Convent (named after the patron saint of Zaragoza in a clear nod to the devotion passed down to María Ignacia de Alzor y Echeverz from her father), with the Mexico *Enseñanza* finally opening its doors on January 11, 1755.

Over the following years, the arrival of the Company of Mary transformed women's education, triggering a true pedagogical revolution.[34] In addition to the quality of the education it provided (which was far superior to that offered by other institutions), the *Enseñanza* was also organized in a singular manner. Its board was made up of members of the founder's family, and it was funded by private donations, which were invested in bonds and real estate to ensure a steady income. In 1811, for example, the *Enseñanza* had annual revenues of 18,990 pesos.[35]

The group of donors included numerous Basques, even though, by that time, that same community had already started to establish its own schools. The relationship between the Mexico *Enseñanza* and the *Vizcaínas* School was somewhat paradoxical, since although there were certain clashes and differences, the two institutions also had many points in common. Indeed, two of the most important founders in the history of the *Vizcaínas* School were very much in favor of the Company of Mary. In addition to donating 4,000 pesos, Antonio Bassoco also assumed the post of trustee during the expansion work carried out at the *Enseñanza*, to which Francisco de Echeveste also donated a further 10,000 pesos.[36]

The principal qualitative leap forward made by the Order, however, was linked to its way of understanding education, or in other words, its teaching model. The novel system distributed girls across different classrooms in accordance with their level of knowledge, an innovation that affected the architectural distribution of the building. "Pupils did not move up a grade by means of an exam, but rather in accordance with a system of contests oriented toward prizes and stimuli." In other words, they were subjected to a test in which they debated a given topic and those who acquitted themselves best, correcting the others, moved up to the next level.[37] The *Enseñanza* model gradually began to spread throughout New Spain, with one of the new schools opened in that region being the *Real Colegio de Nuestra Señora de Gudalupe de Indias* (Royal School of Our Lady of Guadalupe of the Indies).

Founded in 1753 by the Basque Jesuit, Antonio Modesto Ordoñana, heir to another large family fortune, the school taught only indigenous girls from Mexico City, with no Spaniards or mixed-race or black girls being admitted. Sometime later it would be renamed the Royal College under the protection of the monarch Fernando VI.[38]

The school was established to educate those most in need, under a very strict regime. Both the *colegialas*, i.e., those who lived at the school free of charge in exchange for carrying out cleaning, teaching, or care tasks, and the *pensionistas*, i.e., those who paid a fee to attend, received an education based on the needs of the "political life of the West Indies." This basically meant that, in addition to the Catholic catechism (i.e., a moral education in accordance with Catholic values), they also learned to read and write in Spanish, do basic arithmetic, and perform all manner of domestic tasks. One singular element in their curriculum and something "innate to the natives" was the art of grinding chocolate and maize.[39]

Not long after, the *Nuestra Señora de Gudalupe de Indias* School, which, just like the Company of Mary, took inspiration from Jesuit doctrine when establishing its internal rules and regulations, opened its Public School or

Amiga.[40] However, it was not until 1811 that the Company of Mary took charge of this institution. In the meantime, the Basque *oidor*—a judge of the *Real Audiencias and Chancillerías*, originally the courts of the Kingdom of Castile, which later became the highest organs of justice within the Spanish Empire and founder of the *Vizcaínas* School, Francisco Xavier de Gamboa, assumed leadership of the institution and its reform.[41] He was succeeded by another leading member of the Basque elite, Juan Francisco de Castañiza, who was responsible for asking the Company of Mary to found, in the school, the future *Nuestra Señora de Guadalupe y San Luis Gonzaga* Convent, more commonly known as the New *Enseñanza*.[42]

Thus was the role played by certain privileged sectors of Basque origin up until Mexico gained its independence from Spain. After years, centuries even, of fostering the education of New Spanish women under its own set of criteria, the changes that occurred from this time forwards were notable. Many changes had taken place in Mexican society since Father Zumárraga testified before Charles V, the Holy Roman Emperor, and the Council of Trent to the need to protect indigenous girls from pagan practices and polygamy, a custom that was outside Christian law and was deemed an "economic system based on the exploitation of women."[43] At the beginning of the nineteenth century, the arguments employed were rooted in Enlightenment discourses. Juan Francisco de Castañiza justified the founding of the New *Enseñanza* as follows: "there will, in a few years' time, be qualified teachers and useful mothers who will, to a great extent, ensure the happiness of the realm; for said happiness depends on our assets in the West Indies, since they constitute a most principal part of the State."[44]

The prominent role played by those of Basque descent in the development of New Spanish pedagogy, which was mainly due to the fact that they controlled much of the colonial power structures, determined part of their legacy: "From the sixteenth century onwards, the specific interest of the Basques in women's education is indisputable. Throughout the viceregal regime, educational institutions for women and girls in Mexico were closely associated with the patronage of the Basques."[45] And the jewel in the crown of this project was, undoubtedly, the *Vizcaínas* School.

The Origins of the Vizcaínas School

The support mechanisms deployed by Basque men, families, and institutions throughout the early modern period constituted a group/cultural strategy, a way of understanding emigration that held the support provided by Basques to other Basques, whether it be on the grounds of compatriotism, kinship, trust, or friendship, to be a central element of the utmost importance. Galician,

Cantabrians and Catalonians had all behaved in exactly the same way for centuries (see Appendix: Table 1).

The most successful and best positioned figures within these coteries mobilized the rest—"the others from the Basque Nation," as demonstrated by the fact that they gathered every year "on behalf of the Basque nation" to bestow power on two individuals capable of managing, in favor of their "party," appointments to the Trade Consulate of Mexico.[46] The core group of powerful Basques made it their business to protect their fellow countrymen living in the viceroyalty, exercising their leadership, and founding, during the second half of the seventeenth century, the embryo of what would later become the Basque community.

Over the centuries of the early modern period, those hailing from the Kingdom of Navarra, the Señorío de Vizcaya and the provinces of Guipúzcoa and Álava used their influence at the Royal Court as a mechanism for representing and defending their interests to the king, and from the seventeenth century onward, the phenomenon of the national guilds grew stronger. In 1677, the first attempt was made by Basque emigrants to establish, in Madrid, what would eventually become the San Ignacio guild, founded with money from the West Indies: "a quid pro quo at an imperial, transatlantic scale."[47] By that time, Guipúzcoa, Álava and Vizcaya had already begun to define themselves as sister provinces.[48]

Even before that, however, Basque emigrants had reached a notable level of organization, as evident in the foundation of congregations in Seville (1540), Cadiz (1626), and Lima (1635).[49] These were later joined by the Mexican Aránzazu Guild,[50] formed by Navarrans in Madrid in 1648,[51] the aforementioned San Ignacio Guild in 1715, with its "agent in the West Indian office" (i.e., its representative who was exclusively dedicated to dealing with American affairs at the Royal Court[52]) and the Aránzazu Guild of Manila (1749).[53] The founding of these congregations and guilds made the Basques' presence felt in all the major cities of the empire.

Their expansion throughout New Spain is also worth mentioning. Throughout the second half of the eighteenth century, different groups of Basques imitated their countrymen in Mexico City, founding guilds in Guadalajara, Zacatecas,[54] Veracruz, Puebla, and San Luis Potosí.[55]

These institutions were made up of emigrants and their descendants and were designed to offer support and aid to that community. Their liturgical mission also had clear social consequences, since under the auspices of Basque-Navarran devotional figures such as San Ignatius of Loyola, Saint Francis Xavier and the Virgin of Aránzazu, emigrants found a common sense of identity. By celebrating their festivities far from their homeland, they developed strong bonds of social cohesion that set them apart from the rest.[56]

Another aim of these organizations was to deploy certain solidarity mechanisms in the community. The congregations would, for example, cover any funeral costs incurred by an emigrant. However, their principal purpose was to defend their community, acting as lobbies advocating for the Basque political institutions and their rights and privileges, as well as certain individual interests, all at a global scale. This "universal dimension"[57] would eventually help configure a Basque-Navarran "institutional entangled global network" within the Spanish Empire: "In essence, communication and collaboration among emigrants, the associations of countrymen and the authorities in their native homelands help explain the migratory policy of those hailing from the Pyrenees."[58] Taking advantage of this dense network of commercial agents and fellow countrymen, the congregations (with the Madrid-based San Ignacio Guild at the forefront) gained a large measure of influence.[59]

The Mexican Aránzazu Guild was made up of Basque and Navarran emigrants and their New Spanish descendants and only accepted donations from fellow countrymen.[60] Following the same logic that prompted its establishment, the guild had as one of its principal functions serving as a lobby at a global level. This comprehensive outlook, which led to the establishment of firm ties between the Atlantic and Pacific regions, is evident in the foundation of the *Vizcaínas* School, as well as in some of the Guild's business ventures. Up until 1720, for example, its activities were funded by its business interests in the Philippines.[61]

Founded in the capital of the viceroyalty in New Spain, right from the start, the Mexican Aránzazu Guild experienced a number of ups and downs.[62] First established in 1671 as a Fraternity grouping together Basques and Navarrans under the same idol, in 1681 it was incorporated into the San Francisco Monastery, where a chapel was set up in its name. A few years later, in 1696, it became the *Nuestra Señora de Aránzazu* (Our Lady of Aránzazu) Guild and began to arouse suspicion. Indeed, the civil servant responsible for reviewing its rules and regulations sent a request to the archbishop demanding the excommunication of all its members, although in the end the sentence was only carried out in relation to the secretary.[63] As a result, however, the guild requested protection from the king. This was granted in 1729 when the king confirmed its statutes and the organization officially became part of the San Ignacio Guild in Madrid, thereby sharing in all its rights and privileges.[64] It was no coincidence that, three years prior to planning the school, the Basque communities in Mexico and Madrid began to organize themselves and lend each other mutual aid and support.[65]

In relation to its social sway, the guild members enjoyed great influence over the city and its interests. The guild was considered the fourth most important peninsular group in Mexico City, and its weight in the economic life of the region was further increased by its joint control, alongside the Cantabrians, of the Mexican Consulate. The mountain or Cantabrian community shared power in the Consulate with the Basque party. Closely related by family connections, they acted in a similar way. A clear example would be the establishment, as the Basques already did, of scholarships for Cantabrian girls at the Belem school.[66]

The guild's list of members included some of the most powerful clans in eighteenth-century New Spain, such as the Fagoaga family, titleholder to the marquisate of Apartado and owner of one of the largest fortunes in the world at that time,[67] the Castañiza family, the Marquises of San Miguel de Aguayo and the Bassoco family. As well as being the leading advocates of women's education, these families also constituted "a semi-inherited and practically endogamous commercial and business elite."[68]

From a quantitative perspective, the data are very interesting. At the end of the eighteenth century, the guild had 3,087 members, a large number bearing in mind that, during the mid-seventeen hundreds, the Basque-Navarran colony in Mexico City was made up of just 400 families. However, the most significant figure is the fact that, at the end of the seventeenth century, 30.3% of its social mass was made up of women, and by the mid-eighteenth century, "women represented 52.45% of all guild members."[69]

One example of the singular influence exerted by this organization can be found in the support provided to the future large-scale project by the guild's members. Between 1729 (the year in which the king confirmed its statutes) and 1732 (when the project was initiated), two people worked tirelessly to launch the undertaking. These were the sons of a Guipúzcoan and professor at the University of Mexico, Juan José de Eguiara y Eguren, and the descendants of Navarrans, Juan Antonio de Vizarrón y Eguiarreta, Archbishop of Mexico, acting Viceroy, Captain General and President of the *Audiencia*—the name given to an appellate court in Spain and its empire.[70] The governors of the guild together made up the mining, political and financial elite of the eighteenth century.[71]

After a brief survey to confirm the feasibility of the school, the project was finally set in motion in 1732,[72] when the Marquis of Guardiola, a member of the guild and president of the Mexico City Council, intervened in favor of his colleagues to ensure a public transfer of lands for the building.[73] This was one of the few moments of rejoicing the project was to enjoy in a long time, since the magnificent building constructed by the guild over the course of eighteen long years, between 1734 and 1752,[74] would not open its doors until 1767—it was launched with sixty four scholarship girls and six *porcionistas* or interns.[75] In the meantime, some members established scholarships to enable Basque female students to attend Belem School, a move that was a logical solution to the difficulties of the moment. Aware of the delay, the Aránzazu Guild built "four houses and common spaces for the exclusive use of the girls" in Belem.[76]

The building of the *Vizcaínas* School, which cost around 400,000 pesos (other authors will speak of more than half a million pesos[77]) was a titanic undertaking for many of its founders, particularly those who have gone down in history as its three main advocates. For decades, Francisco de Echeveste, Manuel de Aldaco and Ambrosio de Meave—three prototypical emigrants enveloped in the cloak of triumph—constituted the principal driving forces behind the project and were key figures in the influential Basque community settled in Mexico City (see Appendix: Table 2).

Manuel de Aldaco,[78] a native of Oiartzun, Guipúzcoa, and nephew of Francisco de Fagoaga e Yragorri—a knight of Santiago who died in 1736 and author of an economic treaty related to the silver trade,[79] was recruited by his uncle to manage one of the most important emporiums of the Mexican viceroyalty,[80] a post that turned him into the most powerful banker of his time[81] and gained him (among others) the titles of "*apartador general* of gold and silver and Prior of the Royal Tribunal of the Consulate."[82] Thanks to his position as "Purchaser of Silver"[83] and his membership of the Aránzazu Board, the guild's governing body,[84] he held considerable sway over the rest of the community, and was often called upon to oversee the drawing up of wills,[85] as well as to safeguard fortunes[86] and represent different interests.[87] Upon his demise in 1770,[88] he bequeathed the school a total of 66,000 pesos.

Of the famous founding triad, the most influential was Ambrosio de Meave, a rich financier who also occupied important posts in the Mexican Consulate.[89] Born in Durango (Vizcaya), this trader from the world of business and mining[90] proved a key administrator for the future of the school—he donated 36,000 pesos to the school,[91] and was the subject of much praise. His role in the subsequent Mexican expansion of the *Real Sociedad Bascongada de los Amigos del País* (the RSBAP, or the Royal Basque Society of Friends of the Country), the first Enlightenment institution in the history of the Spanish Empire to be founded in the Basque Country, was pivotal. Upon his death he came to occupy a prominent place in the memory of the Bascongada, where a funeral eulogy was read remembering his work.[92]

Years earlier, the first director and founder of the RSBAP, Xavier María de Munibe,[93] represented the province of Guipúzcoa as an agent at the Royal Court.[94] It was there that he came to learn of the San Ignacio Guild, the organization that would prove so useful to him when expanding his Society into the Americas[95]: "The relatives, friends and countrymen of the Count of Peñaflorida planned and developed a transatlantic project that was clearly influential in the economic, social and political development of Hispanic society, thanks to a network of correspondents located in the principal cities of both the Peninsula and the Americas."[96] His uncle, Gaspar de Munibe, Count of Valdelirios, became the principal exponent of Enlightenment ideas in Madrid.[97]

The relationship between these Basque communities was nothing new. After months of maneuvering at the Royal Court in Madrid, in 1753, King Ferdinand VI approved the foundation and constitution of the *Vizcaínas* School under his royal protection.[98] The close relationship cultivated between both brotherhoods led to promote individuals, manage negotiations, and other issues.[99] That same year, the province of Guipúzcoa received some happy news from the San Ignacio Guild: a "celebrated and magnificent school" had been built in Mexico for the "relief and comfort of some boys from these Provinces."[100] Communications were, therefore, obviously effective.

Using preexisting channels of aid and support, the success of the RSBAP was largely due to the participation of its Mexican members, of whom there were around five hundred by the end of the century.[101] And, from 1764 onward, it was the money flowing in from Mexico that enabled much of this dream to come to fruition.[102]

The organization, which has been extensively analyzed by historians, emerges as the last large-scale Atlantic project carried out between the Basque Country and America, a titanic undertaking that stood out, among other things, for the fact that it disseminated scientific and cultural discourses on both sides of the ocean.[103] In pursuit of one of the key reformist concerns of the period, in 1776 it founded what was to become the leading educational and scientific institution of the century, the Patriotic Bergara Seminary, precisely on the site of the old Jesuit school.[104] In other words, part of its success was due to the failure to those who had gone before.[105]

Its New Spanish members came mainly from the Aránzazu Guild, an organization with strong ties to the Court-based San Ignacio Guild and whose relationship with that institution was exploited by the founders of the RSBAP. In 1775, the RSBAP and the San Ignacio Guild, which together formed a conveyor belt linking the two sides of the ocean, joined forces to create a new triangular Atlantic framework.[106]

Figures such as Ambrosio de Meave, who were instrumental to the establishment of the *Vizcaínas* School, also proved pivotal to the successful expansion of the RSBAP in New Spain. "Appointed Commissioner in 1771 [...], right up until his death in 1781, he was a great promoter of the Society and its reformist ideas in Mexico, bequeathing an income of 12,000 pesos to found and maintain two chairs in the Patriotic Seminary of Bergara."[107] Meanwhile, the personal ties between Mexican and Basque members grew closer. In 1781, Meave himself was granted powers to oversee the payment of a debt to be settled in Guipúzcoa in favor of Joaquín de Eguía, Marquis of Narros, one of the most important founders of the RSBAP. This appointment (which was one of many)[108] is a clear example of the trust that existed between the Basques and the Mexicans on both sides of the Atlantic.[109]

The relationships established were mutually beneficial, since just as the Mexican members helped fund the Patriotic Seminary of Bergara, so too did "the Society encourage the establishment of the *Vizcaínas* School."[110] It was no coincidence that the headquarters of the RSBAP in Mexico was located in the *Vizcaínas* School—between 1817 and 1819, to cite an example, the Basque elites of Mexico sent a series of funds to the Bascongada Seminary previously deposited in the *Vizcaínas* patronage.[111] Moreover, some of the leading members of this New Spanish elite, such as José María Bassoco, future founder-member of the Mexican Academy of the Language, were educated at the Society's Seminary.[112]

A proper analysis of the plethora of relationships established between illustrious figures from the Basque and New Spanish communities would require an entire chapter. However, thanks to the studies carried out to date, we are well aware of the vital importance of the RSBAP in the spread of Enlightenment ideas throughout America and the key role played by the elite Basque community centered around both this Society and the Aránzazu Guild. As well as promoting education, they also engaged in a series of reformist interventions in sectors controlled by this community, such as mining, trade, and agriculture.[113] The fact that former teachers at the male Seminary in Bergara moved to Mexico under the sponsorship of these organizations attests to these close ties.[114]

Despite the economic complexities that thwarted the dream of the Aránzazu Guild members, it was another type of setback that eventually delayed the founding of the school. The principal problem was, unsurprisingly, linked to its jurisdiction. The guild had been outside the control of the ecclesiastical authorities since the king had extended his patronage and protection, a situation that the guild members hoped to expand to include their new undertaking. This completely anomalous ambition meant that the *Vizcaínas* School aimed, right from its foundation, to constitute itself as a secular institution outside the influence of the Church. In keeping with this idea, the San Ignacio Congregation in Madrid had already requested in 1734 that the Royal Ministry refrain from intervening.[115]

After months of maneuvering at the Royal Court in Madrid,[116] in 1753, King Ferdinand VI approved the foundation and constitution of the school under his royal protection.[117] From that moment on, "the institution would have absolute independence from the *Real Audiencia* (Royal Court) and other tribunals of the viceroyalty, and [. . .] would answer only to the king, the West Indies Council and the Viceroy, as its representative in Mexico."[118] However, the Church was a key antagonist in the negotiations that lasted for over a decade, negotiations that did not come to an end until 1763, when the Holy Father finally granted the requests formulated by the congregation and the school was officially declared outside ordinary metropolitan jurisdiction—the complex negotiations unfolded in Rome were piloted by the Congregation of San Ignacio under direct instruction of that of Aránzazu.[119] This autonomy from metropolitan canonic law turned the *Vizcaínas* School into the first secular school in the history of the American continent.[120]

Up until its definitive opening in 1767, the school also had to contend with a number of other disputes. The initial attempts made by Ignacia de Azlor y Echeverz, the rich Mexican creole founder of the *Enseñanza*, were aimed at founding the institution on the model of the Belem School or those being built by the Aránzazu Guild in Mexico, an intention conveyed in a letter to the king in 1751. Indeed, "prior to October 1751, the Archbishop of Mexico, Manuel Rubio y Salinas, had sounded out (with negative results) the possibility of establishing a convent in the *Vizcaínas* School." When the Guild Board met in 1752 (the year in which construction work on the main building was completed), they categorically rejected the proposal to turn their project into an *Enseñanza* school.[121] Moreover, in stating their refusal, they also alluded to another attempt made in 1745 by one of the nun's relatives, who offered 70,000 pesos in exchange for permission to establish a convent.[122]

In this context, Manuel de Aldaco's response to Ambrosio de Meave leaves no room for doubt regarding the tense climate that dominated proceedings during that period: "Ambrosio, please find enclosed the response given by the Archbishop regarding the process currently underway to obtain the permission required to open the school. I am also sending a copy to Francisco Xabier de Gamboa and should tell you that, as far as I am concerned, we should deal only with the Court and with Rome (i.e., the Vatican) and if we are unsuccessful, we should burn the school down."[123] We can therefore deduce that one of the most prominent founders would have preferred to see the building in flames rather than in someone else's hands. This series of disputes also affected the Society of Mary in America, since the foundations of Irapuato and Gudalupe knew firsthand the rejection of sectors made up of enlightened politicians and clerics.[124]

The last of the three famous promoters of the school was Francisco de Echeveste, the decorated general in charge of the Philippines Galleons who features so prominently in the founding myth of the *Vizcaínas* School.[125] Consul and Prior of the Royal Consulate Tribunal, he was also governor of the Guild in 1740.[126] However, the most interesting thing about Francisco de Echeveste is the fact that, upon his demise, he bequeathed a minimum sum of 122,000 pesos to the foundation, and, despite all the aforementioned difficulties, a further 10,000 pesos to the Mexico *Enseñanza*.[127]

But General Echeveste represented much more than this. In 1719, he took his first steps in his naval career by serving as captain of (and losing) the Nuestra Señora de Loreto in its expedition to Tonkin, after which he was appointed ambassador of Spain at the court of the Chinese Emperor.[128] After this posting, he began his vertiginous rise in the world of business in the highly profitable Pacific region, and in 1732, founded the Aránzazu Guild in Manila, a move that enabled him to retire in order to establish Casa Echeveste, a company specializing in oriental trade.[129] After moving to New Spain, he came into contact with the Basque colony in Mexico City, where he spent the rest of his days amassing an impressive fortune. Despite his impeccable service record, General Echeveste nevertheless engaged in certain shady dealings, and was sentenced to pay a fine of 4,134 pesos for sending unregistered silver from Mexico to the Philippines (edicts formulated by the Governor of the Islands). Although he was later pardoned in 1761, by that time, he had been dead for eight years.[130]

Silver smuggling in New Spain was a major conflict throughout the Modern Age. The Royal Decree of 1660 was categorical in denouncing that a third of pineapples and *barretones* were contraband, a fraud for which *azogueros*, miners, and royal administrators were identified as responsible.[131] The Basque General was not the exception of New Spain smuggling with the Philippines, take the case of Luis Sánchez de Tagle.[132]

Francisco de Echeveste made his fortune from the Pacific economic circuit controlled by the Mexican Consulate that he would come to know so well, first as a naval officer in charge of its fleet, and later as a trader and consular officer—in 1746 he was appointed universal heir to General Juan de Torres, a native of Hernani, Gipuzkoa, who's fortune was estimated at 14,000 pesos.[133] However, at the same time as he triumphed in the business field and loaned large sums of money,[134] he also increased his charitable work. His reason for doing so was rooted in a very specific feeling of compatriotism: two years before passing away, he founded a collative ecclesiastical benefice of masses that, he stipulated, was only to be managed by legitimate descendants of "*Spanish forebears* [. . .], *excluding any other race, caste or mixture.*"[135] Thus, the benefice of masses, founded in favor of the Aránzazu Guild, had to be managed (in order of preference) by chaplains of Guipúzcoan, then Vizcayan, Alavan, and Navarran descent. According to its founder, beneficiaries of *"any other origin"* were not acceptable,[136] although it should be noted that he was not, by any means, the only rich patron to proceed in such a manner—in 1773 Luis de Oyarzabal appointed chaplains of Basque origin in compliance with the will of Juan José de Aldaco y Fagoaga, who founded six collative chapels with the main one being 4,000 pesos in favor of the Colegio de las Vizcaínas.[137]

This incredible legacy epitomizes his view of compatriotism and charity, key elements in his long and fruitful career. After years of amassing wealth with no one to leave it to, General Echeveste tasked his friends and the executors of his will, Ambrosio de Meave, Manuel de Aldaco and his nephew, Juan José, to distribute his fortune, a decision that most likely turned him into one of the most generous donors of his time. He seemed to have been fully committed to this decision, since he stated that he did not care where he was buried, as long as his friends executed his instructions to the very letter (see Appendix: Table 3).[138]

General Echeveste's actions in favor of emigrants of Basque origin formed part not only of the widespread charity work carried out by the Aránzazu Guild, but its financial operations also. A large percentage of the project costs was covered by pious works and benefices bequeathed by Basques who had emigrated to Mexico, sums that, when invested in bonds, provided revenue used to establish scholarships for young girls. The loans were used to promote or cover the activities of fellow countrymen, who came to the congregation in search of financing (see Appendix: Table 4).[139] These investments were of crucial importance: "In a period in which there were no banks, this provided the Basques with strong economic support, not only as individuals but also as group, which in the eighteenth century, due to the sum of its investment, emerged as the principal driving force behind the New Spanish economy."[140]

The definitive opening of the school in 1767 saw the birth of one of the longest-lasting educational establishments on the American continent, a project that would survive even the confiscations decreed by the Mexican government during the nineteenth century. Melchor Ocampo, one of the main ideologues of the Reform Laws that separated the Church from the State, decreed the following on January 6, 1861 after meeting with José María Lacunza, an influential member of the Aránzazu Brotherhood with numerous friends within the Mexican government: "Being the Colegio de San Ignacio an educational establishment, not ecclesiastical, but merely secular whose patronage formerly resided in the King and now in the Nation, it is declared that the assets that belong to it are not compromised in the Law that nationalized ecclesiastical assets."[141] But, who was the project actually designed to benefit?

LIFE AT THE SCHOOL

Right from the start, the purpose of the school was to provide an education to the daughters and descendants of less wealthy Basque emigrants, and as such, was an institution that was fully consistent with the guild's criteria and philosophy. However, one of the main arguments used by its founders was "propriety," a classist motivation aimed at preserving the good reputation of the community as a whole.[142] As the group of nobles they were, the Basque community saw and built itself on the basis of fundamental elements such as nobility. This is why the founding myth, in which one of these prominent men is said to have been moved upon seeing a Basque girl in difficult circumstances, was not actually that far from the truth:

> upon seeing the extreme hardship suffered by our ladies, maidens and widows, which forces them not only to forsake all self-respect, but also, and more sensibly and pitifully, to relax all manner of customs, thereby leading to notable scandals, pernicious examples and the ruin of the public honesty that should accompany those who, by dint of their ancestors, have notorious obligations and more pressing motives to embrace Christian piety and zeal, and striving to overcome these pitiful disadvantages so that the honor and reputation of their countrymen may remain in their descendants; they determined to found a house or school.[143]

Regarding whom exactly the institution was designed to benefit, the constitution drafted by the Board left no room for doubt: "All must be legitimate Spanish daughters [...] no illegitimate daughters may be admitted, even though they may be recognized by their fathers, nor any Indians, girls of mixed race, Mulattos, Negroes or those of any other Nation, but only Spaniards [...] preference shall be given to the descendants of Basques, be they daughters, granddaughters or of an interior degree."[144] Despite this, however, it was not the descendants of Basques who ended up attending the school, but rather mainly New Spanish Creoles.[145]

The school's regulations or statutes were drafted in 1752 and obeyed the logic of the contemporary context: a secular school governed by the norms of the cloister that took as its reference Belem School, in which the members of the Aránzazu Guild had been intervening for years.[146] With a regime of rigorous retreat from the world—although this goal was not always achieved,[147] the school had guards charged with watching over the outer parlor, a nurse, choir prefects, portresses and those in charge of the revolving hatch, a secretary, a rectoress, a vice-rectoress, and two chaplains.[148] Regarding the educational curriculum, pupils were mainly schooled in strict Christian doctrine, although they also learned how to read, write, do basic mathematics, and perform the "tasks appropriate to their sex."[149]

The XXV Constitution speaks of "the daily distribution for the Christian and Political exercises of the College": "At half past five it will be time to get up. At six o'clock they will be in the Choir to hear Mass and those who remain because they have to occupy each house or College, will hear the second one at [...] From nine o'clock until about twelve o'clock, they will retire to their respective houses, to attend to sewing, needlework, embroidery, reading, and writing or similar honest Exercises. At twelve o'clock the bell will ring for lunch and the inhabitants of each dwelling will eat together and after giving thanks, they will sleep the [...] At three in the afternoon they will return to the maneuvers or sewing until five o'clock in winter and until six o'clock in the summer [...] And every afternoon on holidays, they will be able to go out to have honest fun in the gardens of the College, until the hour calls for the Christian exercises of the Choir."[150]

Several other similar initiatives emerged on the American continent. Despite the distances involved, the territories that, decades later, would become the United States of America, witnessed the development of comparable institutions. Indeed, the process was similar in many ways to that which took place further south on the continent and in Europe, including the initial establishment of small private schools for the young girls of the community, followed by the building (some years later) of large academies or seminaries for women. From the second half of the century onward, wealthier families gradually stopped schooling their daughters at home and began sending them to these new institutions.[151]

In 1727, under the auspices of the French government, the Ursuline Sisters founded in New York one of the first female educational establishments of the region's history, a school that garnered immediate prestige among the local elite, similarly to that which occurred years later with the Mexican *Enseñanza*.[152] Next to emerge were the female academies of Moravia, Pennsylvania (1742), followed by one of the most interesting developments: the Young Ladies' Academy of Philadelphia (1780).[153] Dedicated to educating the most privileged classes, this institution is a good reflection of the major changes that occurred during this period, with young ladies being taught English, mathematics, geography, rhetoric and history.[154] The discourses developed in defense of the "republican mother" by one of the men linked to this academy proved fundamental and was a type of rhetoric rooted in the figure of the European mother/citizen that emerged during the Enlightenment.[155]

In addition to the importance of offering a retreat from the world and its adherence to Ignatian spirituality,[156] three elements stand out in the design of the *Vizcaínas* School. The first was linked to music, a type of instruction that, during the late eighteenth century, became a fundamental part of the most advanced kind of female education, even in the United States of America.[157] The first teachers at the *Vizcaínas* School were recruited from Belem School. They had been trained in their profession thanks to scholarships created by the Basque community at that institution and enjoyed an excellent reputation in the field of music. The *Vizcaínas* School took inspiration from this and maintained close ties with some of the most prestigious musicology studies of the period.[158]

The second element was the importance attached to manual work. One of the principal foundations of the training received by the girls attending the school, in addition to Catholic moral values, was proficiency in household tasks. Pupils were taught how to become good wives in accordance with the criteria of the period, learning skills such as embroidery, sewing, and the decorative arts. So important were these practices that the school even had its own Domestic Duties room.[159]

Finally, the third element was the design or organization of the school itself, which is connected to the two previous elements. Thanks to the influence of Belem School and the importance attached to teaching pupils to be good wives, the young girls attending the school lived in designated dwellings.[160] These dwellings simulated a domestic context and had their own individual rooms, bedrooms, kitchen, and wash house. Overseen by their teacher, "older girls would clean, wash and iron clothes and cook for the group."[161]

As the century progressed, the institution opened its doors to girls from less wealthy families in the city. The public San Luis Gonzaga Schools were housed in an adjoining building and were attended by local indigenous girls. They were based on the teaching model developed by the Mexican *Enseñanza*, in which more veteran pupils taught their younger counterparts.[162] Indeed, this graded system, organized into classrooms and studies of different levels, proved so successful that the *Vizcaínas* School itself was forced to adopt it at the beginning of the nineteenth century, thereby "renewing the entire school structure."[163] But, exactly how many pupils received an education in this impressive building?

It is difficult to calculate the exact number of girls who attended the *Vizcaínas* School. Although we know that, by 1803, a total of 500 girls had attended the public schools,[164] this level of precision is impossible to replicate in relation to the parent institution. We do know, however, that there were two types of pupil: the *porcionistas*, or paying pupils, and those known as *de gracia* or scholarship students.[165] Beyond this, however, the data are unclear.

The fact that many pupils came and went makes calculating their exact number difficult. Some claim that in 1767 (the year in which the school first opened), there were sixty-eight pupils spread across thirteen dwellings.[166] Other sources, however, report that the school was attended by a total of 160 girls throughout the course of the century.[167] And yet others claim that, in 1795, there were between 260 and 300 pupils (both *porcionistas* and *de gracia*) living at the school.[168] Despite this lack of precise figures, an interesting document was found in the school's archive that records the names, entrance and exit dates, and deaths of over 1,000 pupils during the eighteenth century alone.[169]

Beyond the mere fact of its establishment, which alone is incredible enough given that it was the first secular school in the history of America, the constitution of the school also reflects a clash between different models. New Spanish *novatores*—members of a minority group of late seventeenth—early eighteenth century Spanish thinkers and scientists, clashed with members of the Aránzazu Guild, the Company of Mary and the Society of Jesus over control of the large flows of money, political influence, and the expansion of their standards and ideals. And meanwhile, on the other side of the Atlantic Ocean, in the Basque Country, a similar process was also taking place.

NOTES

1   Gonzalo Obregón, *El Real Colegio de San Ignacio de México (Las Vizcaínas)* (Ciudad de México: El Colegio de México, 1949), 46-47; Jesús Ruiz de Gordejuela Urquijo, *Vasconavarros en* México (Ciudad de México: LID, 2012), 198-199.

2   Josefina Muriel, "Las instituciones educativas de los vascos para mujeres de México. Época Colonial," in *IV Seminario de Historia de la Real Sociedad Bascongada de los Amigos del País. "La RSBAP y Méjico"* (Donostia-San Sebastián: RSBAP, Volume I, 1993), 316-423; Josefina Muriel, *La sociedad novohispana y sus colegios de niñas. Tomo II. Fundaciones del siglo XVII y XVIII* (México D.F.: UNAM, 2004); Enrique de Olabarria and Ferrari, *El Real Colegio de San Ignacio de Loyola, vulgarmente Colegio de las Vizcaínas, en la actualidad Colegio de la Paz* (México: Imprenta de Francisco Díaz de León, 1889).

3   Jesús Ruiz de Gordejuela Urquijo, *Vivir y morir en* México. Vida *cotidiana en el epistolario de los españoles vasconavarros 1750-1900* (San Sebastián: Nuevos Aires, 2011); Jesús Ruiz de Gordejuela Urquijo, "Los vascos y navarros en México en el tránsito de la colonia a la nación, 1800-1850," in *Del espacio cantábrico al mundo americano. Perspectivas sobre migración, etnicidad y retorno*, ed. Óscar Álvarez Gila and Juan Bosco Amores Carredano (Bilbao: UPV/EHU, 2015), 249-263.

4   Josefina Muriel, "Los arzobispos vascos y sus obras dedicadas a las mujeres novohispanas," in *Los vascos en las regiones de México. Siglos XVI-XX*, ed. Amaya Garritz (México: UNAM, Tomo IV, 1999), 57-60.

5   Josefina Zoraida Vázquez, "La educación de la mujer en México en los siglos XVIII y XIX," *Diálogos: Artes, Letras, Ciencias Humanas* 17 (1981): 12.

6   Carmen Ruiz Barrionuevo, "Libros, lectura, enseñanza y mujeres en el siglo XVIII novohispano," *Revista de Filología* 25 (2007): 542.

7   Muriel, La sociedad novohispana, 77.

8   Ibid., 73-79.

9   Muriel, "Los arzobispos vascos," 61; Magdalena Ríus de la Pola and Pedro Ramos y Ramos, "El Colegio de las Vizcaínas: una institución vascas en México a través de los siglos," in *Los vascos en las regiones de México. Siglos XVI-XX*, ed. Amaya Garritz (México: UNAM, Tomo III, 1997), 167; Vázquez, "La educación...," 12.
10 Muriel, *La sociedad novohispana*, 85-86; Muriel, "Los arzobispos vascos," 61-62.
11 Muriel, La sociedad novohispana, 80.
12 Fray Luis de León, *La perfecta casada* (Salamanca: Tomás de Alva librero, 1603). See also María Ángeles Cantero Rosales, "De "perfecta casada" a "ángel del hogar" o la construcción del arquetipo femenino en el XIX," *Revista Electrónica de Estudios Filológicos* 14 (2007).
13 Tomás Viejo Yharrassarry, "La segunda dote," *Vasconia* 8 (1986): 31-46.
14 Juan Luis Vives, *La formación de la mujer cristiana* (Valencia: Ayuntamiento de Valencia, 1994).
15 Rosa María Capel Martínez, "Mujer y educación en el Antiguo Régimen," *Historia de la Educación. Revista interuniversitaria* 26 (2007): 86-90.
16 Ibid., 90.
17 Isabel Morant Deusa, "Mujeres ilustradas en el debate de la educación. Francia y España," *Cuadernos de Historia Moderna* III, Anejos (2004): 70.
18 In the inventory of goods that is carried out in her store, in the year 1817, we find the *Catecismo Romano* and *Los Dictámenes del Espíritu*. Sutro Library-California State Library [SL-CSL], SMMS, HG 1:13.
19 José Luis Barrio Moya, "La librería y otros bienes de Doña Ana María de Soroa, dama guipuzcoana del siglo XVIII (1743)," *Boletín de la RSBAP* 47-1-2 (1991): 164-165; Capel Martínez, "Mujer y educación," 91-93; Morant Deusa, "Mujeres ilustradas," 61-64.
20 Molière, *Las preciosas ridículas* (Madrid: Cátedra, 2000).
21 Francisco de Quevedo, *La culta latiniparla*, Biblioteca Virtual Miguel de Cervantes. [consulted the 08/09/17] http://www.cervantesvirtual.com/obra-visor/la-culta-latiniparla--0/html/ffc59bde-82b1-11df-acc7-002185ce6064.htm
22 Muriel, "Los arzobispos vascos," 65-66; Muriel, *La sociedad novohispana*, 89-95.
23 Muriel, "Los arzobispos vascos," 62; Muriel, *La sociedad novohispana*, 86, 115-116.
24 Josefina Muriel, "De Isabel de Urdiñola a María Ignacia de Azlor y Echevers," in *Los vascos en las regiones de México. Siglos XVI-XX*, ed. Amaya Garritz (México: UNAM, Tomo III, 1997), 153; Muriel, *La sociedad novohispana*, 274-275.
25 Donald E. Chipman, *Spanish Texas, 1519-1821* (Austin: University of Texas Press, 1992).
26 María Cristina Mata Montes de Oca, "Mujeres en el límite del periodo virreinal," in *Historia de las mujeres en México* (México: Instituto Nacional de Estudios Históricos de las Revoluciones de México, 2015), 55-59: Muriel, "De Isabel," 155-158; Muriel, "Las instituciones educativas," 414-415.
27 Pilar Foz y Foz, *La revolución pedagógica en la Nueva España (1754-1820)* (Madrid: Instituto Gonzalo Fernández de Oviedo, Tomo I, 1981), 172. The magnificent portrait of Ignacia de Azlor y Echeverz currently belongs to the collection of the Soumaya museum, located in Mexico City.
28 Pilar Foz y Foz and Estela Mejía Restrepo, Fuentes primarias para la historia de la educación de la mujer en Europa y América: archivos históricos de la Compañía de María Nuestra Señora, 1607-1921 (Roma: s.n., 1989), 11-14; Muriel, La sociedad novohispana, 276.
29 Manuela Urra Olazabal, *La educación de la mujer y la Compañía de María en el País Vasco.*

      Siglos XVIII y XIX (Orden de la Compañía de María Nuestra Señora: Ediciones Lestonnac, 2016), 87-88.
30   Ruiz Barrionuevo, "Libros, lectura, enseñanza," 540.
31   Foz y Foz, *La revolución pedagógica*, 44-49 y 79; Muriel, *La sociedad novohispana*, 274-275; Muriel, "De Isabel," 159-160.
32   Mata Montes de Oca, "Mujeres," 57; Muriel, *La sociedad novohispana*, 277-278.
33   Muriel, La sociedad novohispana, 279.
34   Foz y Foz, *La revolución pedagógica*; Muriel, "Las instituciones educativas," 416.
35   Muriel, La sociedad novohispana, 282 y 287.
36   Archivo General de la Nación [AGN], Bienes Nacionales, Volumen 49, Expediente 116. Muriel, "Las instituciones educativas," 415-416.
37   Muriel, La sociedad novohispana, 285.
38   Ibid., 292-295.
39   Ibid., 293-295.
40   Ibid., 293-294.
41   Ibid., 296-300.
42   Ibid., 300-305.
43   Muriel, "Los arzobispos vascos," 58-59.
44   Muriel, La sociedad novohispana, 303.
45   Torales Pacheco, *Ilustrados*, 32.
46   Archivo General de Notarías de la Ciudad de México [AGNCM], Escribano Félix Fernando Zamorano, Notaría 749, Volumen, 5295.
47   Angulo Morales, "Los frutos," 126-128. See also Alberto Angulo Morales, "De la congregación," 199-226.
48   Angulo Morales, "Los hidalgos norteños," 261-296; Alberto Angulo Morales, "De la familia provincial a la atlántica: hijos de las Provincias y Señorío. Reputación y éxito en la movilidad norteña (XVI-XIX)," in *Familias, trayectorias, desigualdades. Estudios de historia social en España y en Europa ss. XVI-XIX*, ed. Francisco García González (Madrid: Sílex, 2021), 179-200.
49   Elisa Luque Alcaide, "Relaciones intercontinentales de la Cofradía de Aránzazu de México," in *IV Seminario de Historia de la Real Sociedad Bascongada de los Amigos del País. "La RSBAP y Méjico"* (Donostia-San Sebastián: RSBAP, Tomo I, 1993), 463-465.
50   Elisa Luque Alcaide, "La cofradía de Aránzazu de México (1681-1861). Continuidad de un proyecto," in *Devoción, paisanaje e identidad. Las cofradías y congregaciones de naturales en España y en América (siglos XVI-XIX)*, ed. Óscar Álvarez Gila, Alberto Angulo Morales and Jon Ander Ramos Martínez (Bilbao: UPV/EHU, 2014), 227.
51   Elena Sánchez de Madariaga, "Caridad, devoción e identidad de origen: las cofradías de naturales y nacionales en el Madrid de la Edad Moderna," in *Devoción, paisanaje e identidad. Las cofradías y congregaciones de naturales en España y en América (siglos XVI-XIX)*, ed. Óscar Álvarez Gila, Alberto Angulo Morales and Jon Ander Ramos Martínez (Bilbao: UPV/EHU, 2014), 25-26.
52   Luque Alcaide, "Relaciones intercontinentales," 463.
53   Antonio García-Abásolo, "Cofradías y hospitales de Filipinas (siglos XVI-XVIII)," in *Devoción, paisanaje e identidad. Las cofradías y congregaciones de naturales en España y en América (siglos XVI-XIX)*, ed. Óscar Álvarez Gila, Alberto Angulo Morales and Jon Ander Ramos Martínez (Bilbao: UPV/EHU, 2014), 75-77.

54 Fréderique Langue, Los señores de Zacatecas. Una aristocracia minera del siglo XVIII novohispano (México: Fondo de Cultura Económica, 1999), 363-364.
55 Torales Pacheco, *Ilustrados*, 30-31.
56 Clara García-Ayluardo, "El milagro de la Virgen. El desarrollo de los vascos como grupo de poder en la Nueva España," in *IV Seminario de Historia de la Real Sociedad Bascongada de los Amigos del País. "La RSBAP y Méjico"* (Donostia-San Sebastián: RSBAP, 1993), 441-443.
57 Luque Alcaide, "Relaciones intercontinentales," 465.
58 Alberto Angulo Morales, "El *institutional entangled global network* de navarros y vascongados en la defensa atlántica por la plata peruana del Seiscientos (Madrid, Potosí y Puno)," *Protohistoria* 35 (2021): 362.
59 Elisa Luque Alcaide, "Recursos de la Cofradía de Aránzazu de México ante la corona (1729-1763)," *Revista de Indias* 56-206 (1996): 213-218.
60 Muriel, La sociedad novohispana, 187.
61 Luque Alcaide, "Relaciones intercontinentales," 477-480; Elisa Luque Alcaide, "Asociacionismo vasco en la Nueva España: modelo étnico-cultural," in *Los vascos en las regiones de México. Siglos XVI-XX*, ed. Amaya Garritz (México: UNAM, Tomo II, 1996), 72.
62 Archivo Histórico del Colegio de las Vizcaínas [AHCV], Estante 6, Tabla I, Volumen 2. Elisa Luque Alcaide, "Investigaciones sobre la Cofradía de Aránzazu de México (siglos XVII-XIX)," *Anuario de la historia de la Iglesia* 2 (1993): 303-306.
63 Muriel, La sociedad novohispana, 187.
64 Luque Alcaide, "Recursos," 205-208; Pedro Ramos y Ramos and Magdalena Rius de la Pola, "Tres momentos en la vida del Colegio de las Vizcaínas," in *Los vascos en las regiones de México. Siglos XVI-XX*, ed. Amaya Garritz (México: UNAM, Tomo IV, 1999), 103-104; José Ignacio Tellechea Idígoras, "La Cofradía de Nuestra Señora de Aránzazu en la ciudad de México (1681-1794)," in *Las huellas de Aránzazu en América*, ed. Óscar Álvarez Gila and Idoia Arrieta Elizalde (Donostia: Lankidetzan, 2004), 44-49; José Ignacio Tellechea Idígoras, *El Colegio de las Vizcaínas de México y el Real Seminario de Vergara* (Vitoria-Gasteiz: Eusko Jaurlaritza-Gobierno Vasco, 1992).
65 AHCV, Estante 4, Tabla V, Volumen 1.
66 Muriel, La sociedad novohispana, 115.
67 Salvador Méndez Reyes, "Los Fagoaga: magnates de las minas Zacatecanas y de la Independencia," in *Los vascos en las regiones de México. Siglos XVI-XX*, ed. Amaya Garritz (México: UNAM, Tomo V, 1999), 297.
68 Leonor Ludlow Wiechers, "Los vascos-mexicanos ante los gobiernos independientes. Relaciones financieras y políticas," in *IV Seminario de Historia de la Real Sociedad Bascongada de los Amigos del País. "La RSBAP y Méjico"* (Donostia-San Sebastián: RSBAP, Tomo I, 1993), 909; David A. Brading, *Mineros y comerciantes en el México borbónico (1763-1810)* (México D.F.: Fondo de Cultura Económica, 2015); María Pía Taracena, "La migración dorada: una familia vizcaína encuentra fama y fortuna en la ciudad de México a finales del siglo XVIII y siglo XIX. El caso de los Bassoco," in *Los vascos en las regiones de México. Siglos XVI-XX*, ed. Amaya Garritz (México: UNAM, Tomo IV, 1999), 220; Verónica Zárate Toscano, "Estrategias familiares de los nobles de origen vasco en la Nueva España," in *Los vascos en las regiones de México. Siglos XVI-XX*, ed. Amaya Garritz (México: UNAM, Tomo II, 1999), 226.
69 Luque Alcaide, "Asociacionismo vasco," 70-71.
70 Tellechea Idígoras, "La Cofradía...," 49; Muriel, "Los arzobispos vascos," 62-69.

71 Brading, *Mineros y comerciantes*, García-Ayluardo, "El milagro," 445; Doris M. Ladd, *La nobleza mexicana en la época de la independencia, 1780-1826* (México: Fondo de Cultura Económica, 1984).
72 Muriel, La sociedad novohispana, 190.
73 Ibid., 196.
74 Manuel Carrera Stampa, "El Colegio de las Vizcaínas. Primera escuela laica en el continente americano," *Memoria de la Academia mexicana de la Historia* 26-4 (1967): 410.
75 Elisa Luque Alcaide, "Autonomía jurídica del Colegio de las Vizcaínas en el siglo XVIII (estudio de unos documentos romanos)," *Anuario Mexicano de Historia del Derecho* 2 (1990): 154.
76 Muriel, La sociedad novohispana, 96.
77 Tellechea Idígoras, "La Cofradía. . .," 49. According to the documentation kept in the Colegio de las Vizcaínas, the equivalent of 8,000,000 Castilian reales. AHCV, Estante 5, Tabla V, Volumen 6.
78 Brading, *Mineros y comerciantes*, 167-168 and 220-271.
79 Archivo Histórico Nacional [AHN], Órdenes Militares, Caballeros Santiago, Expediente 2815; Francisco de Fagoaga e Yragorri, Tablas de las cuentas del valor líquido de la plata del diezmo y del intrínseco y natural de la que se llama quintada y de la reducción de sus leyes a la de 12 dineros (México: Imprenta de José Bernardo de Hogal, 1729). On the important lineage of the New Spain Fagoaga see José Manuel, Azcona Pastor, Possible Paradises. Basque Emigration to Latin America (Reno: University of Nevada Press, 2002), 108; José María Imízcoz Beunza and Rafael Guerrero, "Familias en la Monarquía. La política familiar de las elites vascas y navarras en el Imperio de los Borbones," in Casa, familia y sociedad, ed. Imízcoz, José María (Bilbao: UPV/EHU, 2004), 230-231; Salvador Méndez, "Los Fagoaga," 297-308; Laura Pérez Rosales, Familia, poder, riqueza y subversión: los Fagoaga novohispanos 1730-1830 (México: Universidad Iberoamericana, RSBAP, 2003), 17-50; Juan Javier Pescador, "La familia Fagoaga y los matrimonios en la ciudad de México en el siglo XVIII," in Familias Novohispanas. Siglos XVI al XIX, ed. Pilar Gonzalbo Aizpuru (México D.F.: El Colegio de México, 1991), 203-226; Juan Javier Pescador, Familias y fortunas; Juan Javier Pescador, "The New World"; Javier Sanchiz Ruiz, "La familia Fagoaga. Apuntes genealógicos," Estudios de historia novohispana 23 (2000): 134-135; Juan, Vidal Abarca y López, "La nobleza titulada en la Real Sociedad Bascongada de los Amigos del País," in II Seminario de Historia de la RSBP (Donostia: RSBAP, 1988), 459-461.
80 Sanchiz Ruiz, "La familia Fagoaga," 133-135.
81 Pérez Rosales, *Familia*, 37.
82 Gorka Rosain Unda, "La Cofradía de Nuestra Señora de Aránzazu y los benefactores Aldaco, Echeveste y Meave. Colegio de las Vizcaínas," *Euskonews* (2004). [consulted the 14/09/17] http://www.euskonews.com/0246zbk/kosmo24602.html.
83 AGNCM, Escribano Felipe Romo de Vera, Notaría 591.
84 AHCV, Estante 5, Tabla V, Volumen 7.
85 AGNCM, Escribano José Molina, Notaría 400, Volume 2653. For an approach to the influential Mexican Tagle, Mariano Ardash Bonialian, *El Pacífico hispanoamericano: política y comercio asiático en el imperio español, 1680-1784* (México: El Colegio de México, 2012); Francisco Iván Escamilla González, *Los intereses malentendidos. El Consulado de Comerciantes de México y la monarquía española, 1700-1739* (México: UNAM, 2011); Manuel Rivera, *Los gobernantes de México* (México: Imprenta de J. M. Aguilar Ortiz, Tomo I, 1872), 294-306;

Guillermina del Valle Pavón, *Mercaderes, comercio y consulados de Nueva España en el siglo XVIII* (México: Instituto Mora, 2003), 39.

86 AGN, Real Audiencia, Tierras, Volumen 2800, Expediente 11; Another example in AGN, Real Audiencia, Bienes Difuntos, Volumen 4.

87 AGNCM, Escribano Nicolás Ubaldo Benítez Trigueros, Notaría 79, Volumen 519; AGN, Real Audiencia, Tierras, Volumen, 2504, Expediente 15; AGN, Indiferente Virreinal, Caja 6444, Expediente 027. Ana Guillermina Gómez Murillo, "Análisis de redes sociales en los negocios ganaderos de los condes de San Mateo del Valparaíso y marqueses de Jaral de Berrio. Siglo XVIII," in *Historia y patrimonio cultural*, ed. Manuel Alcántara, Mercedes García Montero and Francisco Sánchez López (Salamanca: Universidad de Salamanca, 2018), 1018-1019; Langue, *Los* señores, 47.

88 Pedro Pérez Herrero, *Plata y libranzas. La articulación comercial del México borbónico* (México: El Colegio de México, 1988), 148; Pérez Rosales, *Familia*, 37.

89 AGN, Gobierno Virreinal, Marina, Volumen 39, Expedientes 80, 81 and 82.

90 Brading, *Mineros y comerciantes*, 152-172 and 241-244.

91 AHCV, Estante 6, Tabla III, Volumen 10.

92 Jesús Héctor Trejo Huerta, "Don Ambrosio de Meave y el paisanaje, lealtad y asistencialismo entre dos instituciones vascas," *Euskonews* (2011). [consulted the 15/09/17] http://www.euskonews.com/0574zbk/kosmo57401es.html

93 Joaquín Iriarte, "Javier María de Munibe e Idiáquez. Conde de Peñaflorida. Fundador de la Real Sociedad Bascongada de los Amigos del País," *Boletín de la RSBAP* 22-2 (1966): 191-214.

94 Alberto Angulo Morales, "Des hommes, des idées, et des ressources: le projet de la *Bascongada* et la Congrégation royale des trois provinces de Cantabrie à Madrid (1713-1775)," in *Savoir et civisme. Les sociétés savantes et l'action patriotique en Europe au XVIIIe siècle*, ed. Michèle Cogriez Labarthe, Juan Manuel Ibeas Altamira et Alain Schorderet (Genève: Slatkine Érudition, 2017), 383.

95 Alberto Angulo Morales, "Embajadores, agentes, congregaciones y conferencias: la proyección exterior de las provincias vascas (siglos XV-XIX)," in *Delegaciones de Euskadi (1936-1975). Antecedentes históricos de los siglos XVI al XIX, origen y desarrollo* (Vitoria-Gasteiz: Gobierno Vasco-Eusko Jaurlaritza, 2010), 72-79.

96 Angulo Morales, "Los frutos," 138.

97 Angulo Morales, "De la familia provincial," 199.

98 AHCV, Estante 5, Tabla V, Volumen 7.

99 AHCV, Estante 5, Tabla V, Volumen 6.

100 Archivo General de Gipuzkoa-Gipuzkoako Artxibo Orokorra [AGG-GAO], JDIM, 4/3/57. Expediente relativo a la fundación del Colegio de San Ignacio de Loyola, para su recogimiento, crianza y enseñanza de 12 niñas pobres y viudas desvalidas españolas en la ciudad de Méjico. Madrid, 10/13/1753.

101 Tellechea Idígoras, "La Cofradía," 49.

102 Cécile Mary Trojani, "Le Collège Patriotique de Vergara et les Amis de la *Bascongada* en Amérique," in *Amitiés. Le cas des mondes américains*, ed. La Promenade (Tensions 1, 2012), 31-44; José Ignacio Tellechea Idígoras, "Socios de la Real Sociedad Bascongada de los Amigos del País en México en el siglo XVIII," in *II Seminario de Historia de la RSBP* (Donostia: RSBAP, 1988), 119-170.

103 Jesús Astigarraga, "Sociedades económicas y comercio privilegiado. La Sociedad Bascongada, La Compañía de Caracas y la vertiente marítima de la Ilustración vasca," *Itsas Memoria. Revista de Estudios Marítimos del País Vasco* 6 (2009): 669-671; Emilio Palacios Fernández, "Proyección de la ilustración vasca en América," *Revista Internacional de Estudios Vascos* 43 (1998): 33-60; Carmen María Panera Rico, "La edad de la Ilustración en España. Lazos de fortuna, devoción y saber entre el País Vasco y América," *Itsas Memoria. Revista de Estudios Marítimos del País Vasco* 3 (2000): 711-727; María Cristina Torales Pacheco "Los socios de la Real Sociedad Bascongada de los Amigos del País en México," in *IV Seminario de Historia de la Real Sociedad Bascongada de los Amigos del País. "La RSBAP y Méjico"* (San Sebastián: RSBAP, Tomo I, 1993), 81-116; María Cristina Torales Pacheco, "Presencia en México de los socios europeos de la RSBAP," in *La Bascongada y Europa. Actas del V Seminario de Historia de la Real Sociedad Bascongada de los Amigos del País,* ed. Guadalupe Rubio de Urquía and María Montserrat Gárate Ojanguren (Donostia-San Sebastián: RSBAP, 1999), 441-462; *La Real Sociedad Bascongada y América* (Madrid: Fundación BBVA, 1992).

104 Álvaro Chaparro Sainz, *Educarse para servir al rey. El Real Seminario de Vergara (1776-1804)* (Bilbao: UPV/EHU, 2011); María Teresa Recarte Barriola, *Ilustración vasca y renovación educativa. La Real Sociedad Bascongada de los Amigos del País* (Salamanca: Universidad Pontificia de Salamanca, RSBAP, 1990); Leandro Silván López-Almoguera, "La Real Sociedad Bascongada de Amigos del País y el Real Seminario Patriótico Bascongado de Bergara," in Historia del País Vasco -siglo XVIII- (Bilbao: Universidad de Deusto, 1985), 175-190.

105 Celia María Aparicio, "Los bienes de los jesuitas en Bergara y el Real Seminario Patriótico Bascongado (Edificios, iglesia y propiedades)," in *II Seminario de Historia de la RSBP* (Donostia: RSBAP, 1988), 257-271.

106 Alberto Angulo Morales, "Las geografías epistolares de las élites vascongadas y la formación de comunidades ilustradas en el siglo XVIII: la Real Congregación de San Ignacio y la Real Sociedad Bascongada de los Amigos del País," in *"Las cartas las inventó el afecto." Ensayos sobre epistolografía en el Siglo de las Luces,* ed. Rafael Padrón Fernández (Santa Cruz de Tenerife: Ediciones Idea, 2013), 69; Angulo Morales, "De la familia," 149; Palacios Fernández, "Proyección," 33-60; Panera Rico, "La edad," 711-727; Torales Pacheco, "Los socios," 81-116; Torales Pacheco, "Presencia en México," 441-462; *La Real Sociedad Bascongada y América* (Madrid: Fundación BBVA, 1992).

107 Palacios Fernández, "Proyección," 37-38. AHCV, Estante 6, Tabla I, Volumen 23.

108 AGN, Real Audiencia, Bienes Difuntos, Volumen 4; AGNCM, Escribano José de Morales Mariano, Notaría 413; AGNCM, Escribano José de Molina, Notaría 400, Volumen 2653; AGNCM, Escribano Juan Antonio de Arroyo, Notaría 19, Volumen 143; AGNCM, Escribano Agustín Guerrero y Tagle, Notaría 268, Volumen 1724; AGNCM, Escribano Vicente José Lanfranco, notaría 651, Volumen 4451.

109 AGNCM, Escribano Mariano Cadena, Notaría 150, Volumen 892. Montserrat Gárate Ojanguren, "El marqués de Narros y el comercio directo con América (utilidad y necesidad del comercio)," in *II Seminario de Historia de la RSBP* (Donostia: RSBAP, 1988), 273-309.

110 Palacios Fernández, *La mujer,* 87.

111 Montserrat Gárate Ojanguren, "Remesas de capitales mexicanos a Europa en el siglo XIX. La participación vasca," in *Los vascos en las regiones de México. Siglos XVI-XX,* ed. Amaya Garritz (México: UNAM, Tomo I, 1996), 288.

112 Taracena, "La migración," 219.
113 Torales Pacheco, *Ilustrados*..., 115-142.
114 Ibid., 136-142.
115 Madrid, 22/10/1734. AHCV, Estante 5, Tabla V, Volumen 7.
116 AHCV, Estante 5, Tabla V, Volumen 6.
117 AHCV, Estante 5, Tabla V, Volumen 7.
118 Luque Alcaide, "Autonomía jurídica," 155-156.
119 AHCV, Estante 6, Tabla IV, Volumen 6.
120 AHCV, Estante 5, Tabla V, Volumen 7. Zoraida Vázquez, "La educación," 14. For a discussion of the process, see Carrera Stampa, "El Colegio," 403-443; Luque Alcaide, "Autonomía jurídica," 151-167; Elisa Luque Alcaide, "El colegio de las vizcaínas, iniciativa vasco-navarra para la educación de la mujer en la Nueva España en el siglo XVIII," in *X Simposio Internacional de Teología de la Universidad de Navarra* (Pamplona: Universidad de Navarra, Tomo II, 1990), 1443-1454.
121 AHCV, Estante 5, Tabla V, Volumen 6.
122 Foz y Foz, *La revolución*, 170-177; Carmen Ruiz Barrionuevo, "Educación, libro y lectura en el siglo XVIII hispanoamericano," *América sin nombre* 18 (2013): 144; Urra Olazabal, *La educación*, 93-94.
123 Carrera Stampa, "El Colegio," 410.
124 Manuela Urra Olazabal, *La Compañía de María en Bergara. Dos siglos de Historia* (Vitoria-Gasteiz: Gobierno Vasco, 1999), 94.
125 Brading, *Mineros y comerciantes*, 152 and 245.
126 AHCV, Estante 6, Tabla III, Volumen 15.
127 Larraitz Arretxea and Mikel Lertxundi, "El patronazgo del General Francisco de Echeveste," *Ondare* 19 (2000): 269-276; Larraitz Arretxea and Mikel Lertxundi, "Los retratos de los fundadores del Colegio de las Vizcaínas en México," *Ondare* 19 (2000): 437-442; Ana Rita Valero de García Lascuráin, Baltazar Brito Gaudarrama and Juan Carlos Franco Montes de Oca, *Don Francisco de Echeveste. Armas y nobleza* (México D.F.: Secretaría de Educación Pública, Instituto Nacional de Antropología e Historia, Colegio de San Ignacio de Loyola, 2015), 13.
128 He will also hold the position of ordinary mayor of the town of Usúrbil. Valero de García Lascuráin, Brito Gaudarrama and Franco Montes de Oca, *Don Francisco*, 11-15.
129 Carmen Yuste, "Obras pías en Manila. La hermandad de la Santa Misericordia y las correspondencias a riesgo de mar en el tráfico transpacífico en el siglo XVIII," in *La Iglesia y sus bienes. De la amortización a la nacionalización*, ed. María del Pilar Martínez López-Cano, Elisa Speckman Guerra and Elisa Von Wobeser (México D.F.: IIH-UNAM, 2004), 190-193.
130 AGN, Gobierno Virreinal, Reales Cédulas Originales, Volumen 81, Expediente 33.
131 AGN, Gobierno Virreinal, Reales Cédulas Originales, Volumen 6, Expediente 83.
132 Guillermina del Valle Pavón, "En torno a los mercaderes de la ciudad de México y el comercio de Nueva España. Aportaciones a la bibliografía de la monarquía hispana en el periodo 1670-1740," in *Los virreinatos de Nueva España y del Perú (1680-1740). Un balance historiográfico*, ed. Bernard Lavallé (Madrid: Casa de Velázquez, 2019), 143.
133 AGNCM, Escribano Juan Antonio de Arroyo, Notaría 19, Volumen 143.
134 AGNCM, Secretario Felipe Romo de Vera, Notaría 591; AGNCM, Secretario Felipe

Romo de Vera, Notaría 591; AGNCM, Secretario Felipe Romo de Vera, Notaría 591; AGNCM, Secretario Felipe Romo de Vera, Notaría 591.
135 AGNCM, Secretario Felipe Romo de Vera, Notaría 591.
136 AGNCM, Escribano Agustín Francisco Guerrero y Tagle, Notaría 268, Volumen 1724.
137 AGNCM, Escribano José de Morales Mariano, Notaría 413.
138 AGNCM, Escribano Felipe Romo de Vera, Notaría 591.
139 Clara García, "Sociedad, crédito y cofradía en la Nueva España a fines de la época colonial: el caso de Nuestra Señora de Aránzazu," *Historias. Revista de la dirección de estudios históricos del Instituto Nacional de Antropología e Historia* 3 (1983): 53-68; García-Ayluardo, "El milagro," 452-455.
140 Muriel, "La sociedad novohispana," 188.
141 Carrera Stampa, "El Colegio," 411.
142 Muriel, "La sociedad novohispana," 196.
143 Archivo Histórico del Instituto Nacional de Antropología e Historia [AHINAH], Fondo Vizcaínas, Rollo 34. Extracted from García-Ayluardo, "El milagro," 449.
144 AHCV, Estante 5, Tabla V, Volumen 7. Obregón, *El Real Colegio*, 170.
145 Muriel, "La sociedad novohispana," 231.
146 AHCV, Estante 5, Tabla V, Volumen 7. Luque Alcaide, "Autonomía jurídica," 153-154.
147 AHCV, Estante 5, Tabla V, Volumen 6.
148 Obregón, *El Real Colegio*, 180-181.
149 Luque Alcaide, "El colegio," 1450-1452.
150 AHCV, Estante 5, Tabla V, Volumen 7.
151 Margaret A. Nash, *Women's Education in the United States. 1780-1840* (New York: Palgrave McMillan, 2005), 35-37.
152 Averil E. McClelland, *The education of women in the United States* (New York: Gerland Publishing, 1992), 123.
153 Ibid., 123.
154 Margaret A. Nash, "Young Ladies' Academy of Philadelphia," in *Historical Dictionary of Women's Education in the United States*, ed. Linda Eisenmann (Westport: Greenwood Press, 1998), 498; McClelland, *The education*, 123.
155 Margaret A. Nash, "Young Ladies' Academy," 498.
156 Muriel, "La sociedad novohispana," 112.
157 Margaret A. Nash, *Women's Education*, 48-49.
158 Muriel, "Los arzobispos vascos," 67; Muriel, "Las instituciones educativas," 410-411; Muriel, "La sociedad novohispana," 240-241; Josefina Muriel, "La música en las instituciones femeninas existente en el Archivo Histórico del Colegio de San Ignacio de Loyola, Vizcaínas," in *Una Mujer, Un Legado, Una Historia: Homenaje a Josefina Muriel* (México: Universidad Autónoma de México, 2000), 221-226.
159 Ríus de la Pola and Ramos y Ramos, "El Colegio," 168.
160 Muriel, "La sociedad novohispana," 215.
161 Ríus de la Pola and Ramos y Ramos, "El Colegio," 168-169.
162 Carrera Stampa, "El Colegio," 413; Luque Alcaide, "Autonomía jurídica," 154; Muriel, "La sociedad novohispana," 247-254.
163 Muriel, "Las instituciones educativas," 416.
164 Muriel, "La sociedad novohispana," 253.

165 AHCV, Estante 6, Tabla IV, Volumen 6. Carrera Stampa, "El Colegio," 412.
166 María Cristina García Vallejo, "El Colegio de San Ignacio de Loyola ante la extinción de la cofradía de Nuestra Señora de Aránzazu, 1861," in *Los vascos en las regiones de México. Siglos XVI-XX*, ed. Amaya Garritz (México: UNAM, Tomo II, 1996), 247.
167 Muriel, "La sociedad novohispana," 228.
168 Ibid., 229.
169 AHCV, Estante 6, Tabla IV, Volumen 6.

PART II

THE EDUCATION OF (SOME) BASQUE GIRLS DURING THE 18TH CENTURY

THE BEGINNINGS

Within the Basque-Navarran context, early solutions for educating children outside the home were developed by towns or local councils, with the effort involving, in addition to finding premises, teachers, and funding, the need to pass the first laws aimed at guiding the instruction provided to children. This is the case of the laws enacted by the Kingdom of Navarra in 1617.[1] Sometime later, in 1631, the first examinations for teachers were established in the same region. Nevertheless, the real impact of these municipal elementary schools was negligible during the sixteenth and seventeenth centuries.

It was only from the seventeen-hundreds onward that a network of municipal teaching spaces began actively to expand, more attention began to be paid to education and the first large-scale educational reforms were carried out. Moreover, the first teachers paid from the municipal coffers date from the seventeenth century, a testament to the slow nature of this process, which did not really take off until the eighteenth century, when, to give an example, an intervention by the Guipúzcoa *Juntas Generales* in 1721 decreed that all towns must have a teacher.[2] These fledgling schools by no means reflected a desire to provide children with a comprehensive education, but should rather be considered places in which poorly trained teachers did their best to impart some measure of knowledge through their lessons, similarly to that observed in New Spain.

The facts and figures linked to this long process leave little room for doubt: "In 1732, some girls' schools were opened and were attended by 36% of the population aged between 7 and 16 years."[3] These numbers also speak to a high rate of absenteeism, in a context in which education was costly, an enormous burden on family finances and, in many cases, completely useless. Most young girls were educated in the family home by their mothers, who imparted both the practical and moral knowledge that would serve as the basis for their daughters' future personal development. Sending a daughter to be schooled by a poorly qualified teacher[4] not only meant having one fewer pair of hands in the house, but was also a major drain on the family income, since teachers charged money for sharing their knowledge, just like tradesmen charged for their goods.

At the end of the eighteenth century, the Basque territories had a total of 347 schools attended by 13,369 boys and fifty-six schools attended by 2,280 girls.[5] In addition to these municipal schools, there were also others founded as acts of charity (in the form of foundations or pious works)—institutions funded by large fortunes that were managed by different council and ecclesiastical authorities. There were also some cloistered convents which (supposedly) offered a high-quality education to their female students. At the end of the century, the schooling rate among girls in Northern Spain was higher than the national average, which indicates the presence of growing concern and the practical absence of this type of institution at the beginning of the century. In Castile, 11.9% of girls went to school, as opposed to 39% of boys.[6] It was a deserted landscape that only began to be fertilized after the advent of new educational trends and thinking.[7]

This precarious situation reveals the complexity of the context, in which families' financial health determined the educational possibilities enjoyed by their daughters. Moreover, it should be remembered that all females were subject to a lowest common denominator, since girls were only educated to fulfill the mandates of their sex, moving from the guardianship of their fathers to that of their husbands. If marriage (the most coveted option) was, for some reason, not possible, women had two other choices: join a religious order or remain a spinster, with this last alternative being the least desirable.[8] The second major pillar of the education available to most women was Catholicism, in particular, everything connected to the role of women as defined by the Holy Scriptures. This education was believed to serve as a true mirror for women's subsequent moral, sentimental, and ideological development.

All the rest was determined by social and economic differences. In addition to the elements mentioned above (Catholic morals and religion, sexual-corporal education, and gender roles, etc.), another fundamental part of the education provided to women was the practical knowledge they were deemed to require in order to carry out their productive and reproductive work in the home—by reproductive work I understand all that work that does not provide emoluments and that is essential for life. Caring for the youngest and oldest, making clothes, feeding or health care, are part of these tasks.[9] This said, not all women were destined to occupy the same position in the world, a distinction that determined whether they were taught to carry out the tasks in question, or merely supervise them. Less privileged girls attended these early public schools only to (in the best of cases) end up assuming responsibility for most household and family chores.[10]

Women from wealthier backgrounds, on the other hand, received a much more comprehensive education at the hands of private governesses, teachers of all kinds and religious orders. At the beginning of the eighteenth century, members of the Basque elite chose to send their daughters to the *Enseñanza* Convent in Tudela or the Santa Clara Convent in Bayonne, on the other side of the French border.[11] Thanks to their social status, in addition to the elements outlined above, these girls also learned how to read and write and, later on in the century, received instruction in new areas such as music and French, which, by then, had replaced Latin as the universal language.

In the region that concerns us here (the Basque provinces and Navarra), there are many instances of women fitting the profile of "a good wife" who managed to accumulate an impressive amount of knowledge. Celebrated ladies such as Catalina Vélez de Guevara, Countess of Oñate—with a library that had more than 600 volumes in the seventeenth century,[12] Ana María de Soroa, a native of the town of Usurbil and owner of a magnificent library during the early eighteenth century and María Antonia de Salcedo y Chávarri, from the city of Vitoria, first Marchioness of Montehermoso and governess to the future King Louis I,[13] are clear examples of this privileged group of women. According to studies, few large libraries were concentrated in the north of the peninsula at the end of the seventeenth century. While the library industry was weak, approximately 40% of the Spanish population did not speak Spanish.[14]

The first school for girls was established in Bilbao in 1732. That same year a similar process occurred in the small Guipúzcoan town of Bergara. Everything started with a nun called Clara de Berroeta who, in that year, requested permission from the town leaders to go into retreat in the dwelling that had begun to be built next to Soledad Chapel. In exchange for occupying the space, which belonged to the municipality, Clara de Berroeta, a nun of the Third Order of

Saint Francis, offered to teach the daughters of Bergara (girls and women) to read, write, and perform all manner of manual tasks, as well as, of course "to care for and preserve Christian customs."[15] Thus the Bergara Soledad Seminary was founded, which, alongside the Bilbao school, was the first institution of its kind in the history of the Basque Country dedicated to the education of women.[16]

The seminary was soon to start facing problems. The first was linked to the lack of space, a problem that the nuns who accompanied Clara de Berroeta tried to solve by using their own money and future donations to enlarge the premises. However, the most serious problem was connected to the gradual breakdown of unity among the sisters, quarrels that eventually necessitated direct intervention by the seminary's patron, the town of Bergara. By 1739, the seminary was considered "a house of education for Noble Ladies," providing an extremely useful service, since it was attended not only by seminarians who lived there full-time, but also by half-boarders and other girls and women of the town who attended classes on a daily basis.[17] In that year, the Bergara council commissioned Alonso María de Munibe e Idiáquez, the Marquis of Rocaverde and Manuel de Leizaola y Lili (all three of whom had direct ties to the circle of Enlightenment thinkers who, years earlier, had founded the RSBAP) with establishing a set of rules and regulations for the seminary to help solve its problems. The lack of internal regulations and an authority figure to govern the pious was seen as the origin of everything. Such is the case that an attempt was made to extract from the constitutions that governed the Teaching of Tudela the new regulations for the Seminary of Soledad de Bergara, flatly rejected by the devout. The three men in turn charged the famous Jesuit, Manuel de Larramendi, with this task.[18]

The constitution written by Father Larramendi, which was approved in 1741, was a product of its time. In other words, it clearly reflected an educational model based on the more traditional ideas of the era, although it also incorporated some novel elements. Its principal aim was to train good Christian women with "a great appreciation for the things of heaven and a high degree of contempt for those of the century."[19] As regards structure, the constitution stated that the seminary should be organized as a religious community, including a Mother Superior, a minister and a procurator appointed by the town and confirmed by the bishop. The main difference in comparison with other convents lay in the hiring of teachers, with pupils being accepted either as full-time boarders or under semi-cloistered conditions. Father Larramendi's decision to opt for this convent-based organizational regime was linked to his own experience as a reformer "of the Carmelite nuns in Zumaya and the Augustinian nuns in Hernani, San Sebastián, Mendaro and Motrico."[20] A number of points should be highlighted in relation to the curriculum. First, its fundamental aim was as follows:

> "the service of God and His greater glory, and the public utility of all this Country and its surrounds. The means for achieving this is the Christian education provided to the girls who come to the Seminary, coupled with diligent upbringing and instruction designed to cultivate and adorn them with the skills necessary to their sex, as well as with those that will prove useful and will serve to embellish and ornament."[21]

Designed to educate the most privileged classes in conditions similar to those of a convent, instruction also included classes in reading, writing, spelling, basic mathematics, sewing and manners—all within a strict Christian framework. The seminary also taught Latin, as far as possible, and offered classes in singing and music, activities that were very much in vogue during that century, but were still considered acceptable for young ladies. And since most pupils were indeed ladies, the Spanish language also occupied a fundamental place in the curriculum, since it was viewed as the language of the vast Spanish Empire and a vehicle that would open the doors to preferential treatment—"they commonly spoke no other tongue, either with their teachers or among themselves."[22]

Despite all these efforts, however, the constitution of the Soledad Seminary in Bergara was never fully approved. Although it was ratified by the town council and the nuns themselves, authorization from the prelate never arrived. Clara de Berroeta, the founder of the seminary, accepted the constitution, rejecting the council's authority and seeking the protection and patronage of the bishop, thereby paralyzing the entire process. In light of this complicated situation, in 1749, Miguel José de Olaso, procurator general of the town and future founder of the RSBAP, suggested following the advice of Father Larramendi and donating ownership of the seminary to the bishopric of Calahorra, a proposal that was immediately acted upon—in fact, he came to criticize Blessed Berroeta for her attitude.[23] Consequently, ten years later, in 1751, a new constitution was drawn up, this time by another well-known Jesuit, Father Calatayud. Based on the previous document, the main modification had to do with the management of the school, with a clergyman being appointed as director instead of the prelate.[24]

A comparison between the two constitutions reveals very few changes. In response to the school's rejection of physical punishment and other issues that could be seen as novel, such as singing and music classes, Father Calatayud observed that "after so many years without an adequate government and bearing in mind that the seminary is in danger of being lost due to the *caprices of women*, it was decreed that there should be a director appointed by the bishop."[25] It was a turbulent time for the project. The promise it seemed to hold in 1732 had long since faded, and the first women's education institution in the history of the Basque Country was faced with an increasing number of problems. And, most amazingly, we have the very similar story of the *Vizcaínas* school, which was founded in the exact same year.

Bergara as the Center of Everything

The disputes in New Spain were just the preamble to a much larger struggle. The true catharsis was centered around the Guipúzcoan town of Bergara, where there was a constant clash between different and irreconcilable mindsets. With the arrival of new schools of thought linked to the Enlightenment, the standards for women's education underwent a process of transformation that generated a certain amount of friction. Women's education, which was a pressing concern during this period, served as a backdrop, a stage if you like, for the confrontation between two models since, although intentions on both sides seemed honest enough, the coming battle would inevitably end up destroying part of their dreams.

In 1762, the Soledad Seminary in Bergara was experiencing a certain degree of financial hardship, problems which disappeared overnight when the heiress of a rich factor in the service of the *Real Compañía Guipuzcoana de Caracas* (RCGC), the first joint-stock company in the history of the Spanish Empire, founded by Basque traders with the aim of gaining a cisatlantic monopoly over trade with America,[26] decided to donate her entire fortune to founding a school for girls.

This resulted in over a million *reales* being earmarked for women's education at the heart of the Basque Enlightenment, thanks to the generosity of Magdalena de Goizueta Van Breuseghem, a native of San Sebastián and daughter of the controversial factor in the service of the RSGC.

Himself born in Navarra, Juan Manuel de Goizueta y Echeverz worked for the RCGC for years—we do not know if he was related to the founder of the Enseñanza de México, María Ignacia de Alzor y Echeverz, first as master of the San Joaquín, one of the first three vessels chartered to sail to Venezuela, and later as a factor at the company's headquarters in Guaira and Caracas ports.[27] His scandalous fortune, however, was rooted in abuse. In 1749, the Governor of Caracas identified him as one of the people responsible for provoking the uprising against the RCGC in Venezuela led by Juan Francisco de León.

"He complained expressly of Juan Manuel de Goizueta, of whom it was said that he would pay little heed to the orders of the governor or the Royal Offices and would violate the Company contract by dispatching vessels from one port to another, without bothering to inform the fiscal employees of such undertakings or to obtain a permit; he would not even wait for an inspector to board for the journey. 'Goyzueta acted on the basis of his own will and personal criteria ... for him, no other authority existed'. He also notes that the man had distinguished himself for his abnormalities and infringements during the rebellion."[28]

Indeed, the reasons for the unrest in Venezuela seemed evident: "the tough, ardent nature of the principal factor, Juan Manuel de Goizueta, and all the suffering that he, and his dependents, inflicted on those people with their bad terms and irregular practices, made them odious and loathsome."[29] This was the origin of the million or so *reales* he managed to amass during this lifetime.[30]

Her father passed away when Magdalena de Goizueta was just six years old, and a short time later, when she had just turned twelve, she lost her mother also. That is how fate took her to the center that the Company of Mary had in Navarra, the *Enseñanza* Convent of Tudela.[31] The parallels between Magdalena de Goizueta and Ignacia de Alzor y Echeverz, founder of the Mexico *Enseñanza*, are inevitable, since in addition to the fact that their lives followed a very similar course, it is more than likely that Ignacia's achievement served as an example for Magdalena. Just one decade after the New Spanish sister had joined the convent, she was joined by her fellow sister from Guipúzcoa.

Upon taking her vows in 1762, Magdalena was convinced of her vocation to remain with the order. She donated her enormous inheritance, which she would be forced to renounce when she became a nun, to the founding a new convent of the Order of *Nuestra Señora de la Enseñanza* (Our Lady of Teaching), belonging to the Company of Mary, on the site of the old *Seminario de Niñas Educandas de la Soledad* (Soledad Seminary for Female Pupils) in Bergara. The fortune used to establish the school, much of which came from her father's smuggling and pillaging activities, included thirty-six shares in the RCGC, various houses and mansions, deeds, loans extended in Caracas and eighty-four thousand *reales* invested in the *Compañía de Comercio de las Indias Orientales* (East Indies Training Company) in the city of Rouen. The seminary also had 16,000 pesos invested in thirty-two actions of the La Habana Company,[32] a circumstance that saved it from becoming an act of decadence.[33]

Despite her honest intentions, the first problems arose with this very act of relinquishing her fortune, which not everyone in her environment looked upon with favor. When, at the age of the fifteen, she decided to take the veil in the Company of Mary, her relatives and legal guardians intervened and tried to remove her from the convent due to doubts regarding the existence of any true vocation—a conflict suffered also by Ignacia de Alzor.[34] Two of her tutors, priests in San Sebastián and Valladolid, doubted the quality of her vocation and suspected that she had been coerced by the nuns in Tudela.[35]

Eventually, however, her choice was respected and her fortune was donated to founding the new school, a project in which the Society of Jesus played a key role, since one of its members was instrumental in bringing it to fruition. The Jesuit Francisco Mucientes, who was a guest at Tudela during that period, intervened directly on behalf of the Bergara foundation and the dean of the school the Society had in the Guipúzcoan town was appointed Magdalena's executor, alongside the mayor, Miguel de Olaso y Zumalabe, the future secretary of the RSBAP.[36]

Let us keep in mind that "the Ignatian spirituality adopted by the Company of Mary, the Constitutions taken from the Summary of the Jesuits and the close relationship between the members of both Companies from the beginning, led to the fact that, traditionally, the Company of Mary founded in places where there was a Jesuit presence. Bergara had a Jesuit college since 1593."[37]

Although the townsfolk greeted the foundation of the first convent dedicated exclusively to teaching women and girls in the history of the three Basque provinces with enthusiasm, the town's mayor did not appear to share their eagerness. During the thirty-seven years that the Bergara *Enseñanza* had to wait before it was allowed to open its doors, Magdalena's dream languished in endless bureaucracy, victim to the mayor's inactivity. Thanks to the profuse correspondence exchanged between Magdalena and Miguel de Olaso y Zumalabe, we know that the would-be founder accused the mayor of apathy to her cause due to his being so committed to the Enlightened era projects of the RSBAP. She also accused him of being "a declared enemy of the black robes" and of prejudicing the goods he was charged with overseeing. Upon his demise in 1772, he left a debt of 36,895 *reales de vellón* on the bequest that he had used to purchase a living for his sons, one as a soldier and the other as a student.[38]

In the meantime, the *Real Sociedad Bascongada de los Amigos del País* (RSBAP) was founded in 1764.[39] Established in the province of Guipúzcoa, its principal promoters were members of the Basque social elite and included figures such as Xavier María de Munibe, Count of Peñaflorida, the Marquis of Narros, Pedro Jacinto de Álava, Félix María de Samaniego, Manuel Ignacio de Altuna and, of course, Miguel de Olaso, mayor of Bergara in 1767, secretary of the RSBAP and promoter of the Bergara Cutlery Company, a project aimed at reconciling the interests of the RSBAP and the RCGC, two institutions that did not seem to relate in the most satisfactory way.[40]

But what, exactly, did the *Enseñanza* project entail? Magdalena de Goizueta was very precise in her indications: it was to be a convent built in the image and likeness of the one in Tudela, but in the town in Bergara. If either of these conditions were not met, all the monies were to be returned to the Navarran institute. Thanks to these conditions, the future convent would have the classic structure developed by the Company of Mary.

During the endless bureaucratic struggle that preceded its foundation, the Council of Castile ordered the Guipúzcoa magistrate, the Bishop of Calahorra and the members of the RSBAP to voice an opinion regarding its establishment.[41] It was September 5, 1774, and the true disagreements regarding the project were about to emerge. Members of the Enlightened Basque elite intervened to change the playing field,[42] due to the emergence of new approaches to women's role and education.

The Count of Peñaflorida, the first director of the RSBAP, oversaw the formulation of a response to a request he considered to be of the utmost significance, since it was the first time the Crown had called upon the Society for an opinion. Since the request was limited to the drafting of a report, the question had to be resolved in a simple manner, although in truth the issue was infinitely more complex. In the first draft of his report, entitled "B" (document "A" was the Council's Royal Decree), Munibe expressed his views on what the RSBAP's response should be.[43]

His reflections were centered around multiple different ideas. First, he was concerned about the impossibility of modifying any detail at all of the express desires of the founder. Moreover, in the absence of a Confiscation Act, the State could not use the monies as it saw fit, an observation closely connected to the other two arguments. Finally, he recognized the variety of different opinions that existed among the RSBAP's members regarding secular education and the aims of teaching in general, since many were in favor of instruction aimed at raising "Mothers and Wives who, due their sound education and virtue, would contribute to the happiness of the World," as opposed to the "nunnish" education they accused the Company of Mary of providing. In light of this, Munibe reached the conclusion that the members of the RSBAP had a problem, since if they argued that the teaching provided by the Company of Mary was totally harmful, they ran the risk of being rejected in the Basque Country for permitting the fortune and the foundation of the school to be diverted to Tudela.

The solution was to present a Bull approving the foundation of the *Enseñanza* that enabled the hiring of secular teachers, a move that would bypass "the Monastic and anti-Monastic opinions" of the Society's members. This response would enable an education more in keeping with the RSBAP's interests, would free them from complaints, yet would enable them to comply with their obligations to the Council. And all this could quite literally be done with no moral scruples.[44]

The process was not resolved immediately, and the Count of Peñaflorida drafted a new report, entitled document "C," in collaboration with the members from Álava and Vizcaya (the RSBAP was divided into three commissions, one for each Basque territory, as well as its delegations at Court and in America). This new document endorsed the usefulness of the institution, an *Enseñanza* dedicated to educating privileged ladies and the other girls of the local area. The only concerns expressed were linked to the space, since in all else, this second report meshed with the desires expressed by the founder. Right at the end, the document reminded readers that if Magdalena's wishes were not respected, her fortune would end up in Tudela, to the detriment of Basque families, who would have no choice but to send their daughters to Navarra or France.[45] But not everyone agreed with this moderate stance, which prompted the Society to draft a new report, this time entitled document "D."[46]

Document "D" was drafted by the Álavan members of the RSBAP in response to the previous one, calling for aid upon Pablo de Olavide, the famous scholar of Basque origin born in Lima.[47] Much more expeditious than their director,[48] the Álavan members advocated for the manual training of the least advantaged classes, an education that would include trade skills and manufacturing techniques designed to enhance the region's industry and economy.[49] This, according to the Álavan commission of the RSBAP, was the course that should be taken by the future *Enseñanza*.

This more utilitarian approach was due to the influence of the "Olavide report," which constituted the cornerstone of the RSBAP's program of reforms. Meanwhile, some members of the Society had already formed a very clear picture of the right road to take, even before the publication of the Royal Decree. Pedro Jacinto de Álava, head of the Álavan group, was a close friend of Olavide, whom he asked for help.[50] The illustrious thinker from Lima had participated in the drafting of the report for the *Casa de las Becas* at the *Seminario Real de Educandas* in Seville, a copy of which he sent to his Álavan colleagues and which served as inspiration for the rest.[51]

Olavide's proposal, originally drafted in 1768 while he was an Assistant in the city of Seville following the expulsion of the Jesuits, proved paradigmatic of the new ideas emerging regarding education.[52] The seminary he imagined was designed to serve distinguished women destined to "play subsequently in the World a more brilliant role"—"To whom it is therefore important to have a higher education, acquiring from the practice of religion the use of domestic virtues and the tasks proper to the whole sex, the graces, the talents, the instruction that today the century needs to sustain its character with decorum."[53] Criticizing the lack of women's education, which, according to him, was the most necessary thing for the country, he claimed that "no one ever thought to educate a Mother, much less a Lady who, placed in high dignity, illustrated the brilliant virtues of her state."[54]

Olavide censured the fact that wealthy women were educated in convents only to end up taking the veil, a circumstance that was detrimental to the State. If the most distinguished women were educated in the most dignified parameters, men would be forced to change their attitude in order to please them, due to the "atrocious influence and powerful ascendancy" women had over them. Finally, he claimed that women's education (which reached its highest level when imparted by mothers) was the surest means of achieving universal education, particularly among the nobility, in accordance with the tone of the century, a fact that justified the need for education to be provided by the State.[55] The principal points of the plan proposed a deep-rooted change in outlook, an innovative reform that perfectly summed up the Enlightened interests of the period:

"Train them in spirit and heart, and instill in them the respect and obedience they owe to the Government and their Parents: The care they should take in protecting their reputation, living with honor and decorum: Respect, obedience and the art of pleasing their Husband; in short, all the virtues that a Daughter, a Wife, a Mother and a Lady should possess. Moreover, they should be taught the external graces so becoming to their sex, and be instructed in how to preserve them in order to avoid the dissatisfaction that so often arises in Matrimony as a result of their absence."[56]

Designed to accept all those girls who could afford to attend, with no heed being paid to pureness of blood or nobility, the seminary would offer the classic lessons in catechism, manual tasks, reading, writing and basic arithmetic. In a reformist vein, the proposal also included drawing, declamation (the art of speaking), dancing, music, Spanish grammar, French, geography and history, and for more veteran pupils, a smattering of cosmology and poetry. It was a more advanced view of women's education, an elite school which would lack for nothing and would reject austerity in order to serve the interests of women destined to live in the new century—the students could also have a private maid at their service.[57]

The Lima-born thinker did not respond to his colleagues' request until February of the following year, a delay that further prolonged the process.[58] It was only after his response was received that report "D" was drafted by the RSBAP.[59] This report initiated a round of consultations within the Society, resulting in a final report in response to that drafted by the Álavan members.[60] Between the voicing of different opinions and the casting of votes, time continued to transpire until eventually, the final document (document "E") was drafted.[61]

In chronological order, a young Samaniego (who was barely twenty years of age at the time) voted to admit secular teachers, complaining of the lack of education oriented toward all states.[62] The next member to voice his opinion was his uncle, the Count of Peñaflorida, who claimed that the education provided by religious orders to "young ladies of distinction" needed to be vastly improved. Indeed, he undertook not to send any of his daughters to the Tudela convent after having been informed of the inferior quality of the institution. He also argued that the Company of Mary's constitution allowed for the hiring of secular teachers, which he advocated as a splendid idea. Finally, he also stated that: "The Council should, as a general principle of Policy, reject all foundations by a Religious Community."[63] The opinions voiced by Narros,[64] Olaso[65] and the Marquis of Rocaverde[66] proposed similar arguments, a round of declarations that ended with the support of the Álavan members.[67] The definitive report was approved one day later.[68]

This report (document "E") was the most heavily influenced by Olavide's ideas.[69] The undeniable similarities between the two drafts are reflected in the following points: one of the teachers, for example, should help the director in the role of supervisor of manual labors and fashion, all oriented toward training future mothers. Furthermore, each pupil would be able to take a maid with them and all would eat at tables similar to those found in private homes and separately from the nuns, in order to educate them in family customs and habits. The greatest similarities between the two documents, however, lay in their discourse, with the definitive report's focus on the need to educate good mothers and wives being a practical copy of that stated in Olavide's document, with concepts such as civility, good manners, decorum, the distinction of young ladies and their education for the world being amply developed from the time the report arrived in the Basque Country.[70]

The approval of the final report put an end to months of musings, a time during which the true postures of the Society's members (some of which were profoundly anti-clerical) came to light. However, the definitive response sent to the Council (document "E") concealed one of the RSBAP's age-old desires, an ambition the members did their very best to hide. In order to achieve their goal, the members of the RSBAP were willing to offer up their Patriotic Seminary of Bergara, the jewel in their Enlightenment project, as the site of the new center for women's learning.

Since 1767, they had been aware of the possibilities opening up after the expulsion of the Society of Jesus, a situation of which they took advantage to found the Seminary in 1776. It was here that the core of the Basque Enlightenment movement developed most of its educational standards (directed at men only).

In 1765 they gained approval for the Student Regulations[71] and in 1769 (just two years after the expulsion edict), they received permission from Carlos III to occupy the old school that the order had in Bergara.[72] It was in the eight years that passed between this moment and when the school finally opened that the aforementioned events regarding the *Enseñanza* transpired. It was a period in which the Basque Enlightenment movement viewed with a certain degree of cautious hope the possibility of achieving their greatest wish: to occupy the Loyola Sanctuary located just two kilometers from Azcoitia, the residence of the principal promoters of the RSBAP and home to Saint Ignatius of Loyola.[73]

One of the original projects explored the possibility of opening up said seminary in Vitoria. Thanks to a letter written by the Viscount of Ambite to the Count of Peñaflorida in the summer of 1767, the year of the expulsion, we know that the Mayor of Vitoria held a secret council meeting to petition the Royal Court to establish a Seminary for Noble Boarders in one of the buildings abandoned by the order.[74] According to the king's mandate, any building left uninhabited following the expulsion could be used to establish Conciliar Seminaries, Seminaries for Noble Boarders and Schools for Distinguished Young Ladies (as in the case of the Seville seminary in whose foundation Olavide was instrumental). The project, however, never came to fruition.

The proposal made in report "E" of 1775 was simple: providing the nuns were willing to cover the cost of the renovations made by the RSBAP to the Bergara seminary, they were welcome to occupy it.[75] It was an attempt to force the situation and pave the way for them to occupy Loyola, thereby fulfilling one of their oldest dreams.[76] Commissioned in Madrid to process the founding of the Seminary one year earlier, Pedro Jacinto de Álava wrote the following to his friend, the Count of Peñaflorida:

"The affair of the Seminary will come out soon because O'Reilly has undertaken to visit the council members responsible for dealing with it. Urbina [a founding member of the RSBAP], who was yesterday at the site and was charged with finding out from Campo [Campomanes] the situation regarding Iranda's proposal, informed me that [. . .] if we were to substitute the Bergara School for that of Loyola, there would be no difficulty."[77]

Four days later he stated that "Valle Salazar has undertaken also to push forward the business with the Seminary that I spoke of yesterday with your uncle Valdelirios, and he looks favorably on the change to Loyola, if it can be achieved."[78] The goal finally seemed to be in sight: "A certain Countryman who is not a member told me yesterday that he had asked Campomanes why we were simply not given the Loyola School, and he replied that it was because we had not asked for it."[79]

Despite their best efforts, however, it was not to be, mainly because Magdalena de Goizueta emphatically opposed the plan proposed by the RSBAP. From that moment on, the Basque Enlightenment movement was excluded from the future

Enseñanza. It was 1775 and problems multiplied for all parties concerned, especially for the RSBAP, which experienced a personal clash between its director and Pedro Jacinto de Álava, head of the Álavan group.[80] The Society survived, however, and a few months later had joined forces with the San Ignacio congregation in Madrid, as it had with the Aránzazu guild years earlier—in addition to the union between institutions, including the relationship between its partners, it should be noted that the Bascongada had funds invested in the Brotherhood of Aránzazu and the Bank of San Carlos.[81] One year later, in 1776, the RSBAP seminary opened its doors in Bergara.[82]

The disputes which occurred between Mexican *novatores* of Basque origin (later affiliated with the RSBAP), the Company of Mary, the Society of Jesus and members of the Basque Enlightenment movement reflect this conflict. The belief held from very early on by the elite Basque community in Mexico, namely that religious institutions should provide a secular education (understood as religious but emancipated), was strengthened after the Jesuit expulsion. The Enlightenment projects that flourished from that moment onward in societies such as the RSBAP were committed to improving education for the elite, a substantial change that strove to respond to an old concern with a new approach: whereas, during the early decades of the seventeen hundreds, there was a general recognition of the need for better education, particularly for women, toward the final decades of the eighteenth century, different specific proposals were being designed on the basis of the ideas developed by the Enlightenment.

The Basque Enlightenment movement viewed women as perfect ladies destined to occupy a prominent place in the world. From this moment on, new gender stereotypes and roles were debated in an attempt to construct a new femininity.[83] The standard for women's education represented by the Bergara *Enseñanza* therefore clashed with the plans of Olavide and his Basque colleagues. And in the midst of all these disputes there was the figure of Magdalena de Goizueta, protagonist of the dramatic story of a nun who died four years before the Bergara *Enseñanza* finally opened its doors in 1799. Magdalena did not survive long enough to see her dream come to fruition, although as with its counterpart in Mexico, the institution she founded still survives today.[84]

THE LAST GREAT DREAM OF THE COUNT OF PEÑAFLORIDA

It was June 25, 1784, when the Count of Peñaflorida, alma mater of the RSBAP, confessed the following: "Although I am fully aware of how little dreams are worth, I would like to tell you mine."[85]

Xabier María de Munibe, founding member and director of the RSBAP, shared a cherished goal with one of his closest colleagues, Pedro Jacinto de Álava, from Vitoria: to found, in the province of Guipúzcoa, a secular, elite establishment for the daughters of the local nobles. "But, what is the point of thinking about this? Where can we find the means to fund in the Basque Country an Establishment of this nature? Here is where my Dream comes in."[86]

The rejection of convent education by the director of the RSBAP was based on sound arguments, at least since his uncle, Gaspar de Munibe, had appraised him of the education provided by the Tudela *Enseñanza* (this occurred in 1773, a couple of years before he pronounced his stance in relation to the Bergara establishment)—educated by the Jesuits, the Count of Peñaflorida would have maintained a good relationship with the order, a feeling that, according to Gabarain, he will not share with the Company of Mary.[87] In Gaspar de Munibe's opinion, girls were educated to become nuns and emerged from the institution "shrunken and with no idea of how to run a household," an opinion shared by the father of the writer of fables, Félix Ignacio Sánchez de Samaniego y Munibe, who once wrote: "after 8 years of cloister life, my younger daughter, who is around 15 years of age, cannot read or sew anything more than would be expected of a young girl."[88] The Enlightened Basque elite were therefore faced with the inconvenience of having to send their daughters to either Tudela or France.[89] As a result of his disapproval of the Navarran institution, the Count of Peñaflorida sent one of his daughters to the Santa Clara Seminary in Bayonne; hence the potential importance of the Bergara *Enseñanza* for the future of the region.[90]

Concern over women's instruction, which was viewed as fundamental for universal education, was reflected in the constitution of the RSBAP itself. One of the four solemn speeches made during the opening celebrations of the RSBAP in 1765, given by the Marquis of Montehermoso, focused exclusively on this issue.[91] Entitled "A Philosophical-Moral Discourse. Women,"[92] it highlighted "the inequality of the sexes, from which we can deduce the different social function of each; asserted the generalized opinion of society that nothing that requires strength or reflection should be destined for women, but rather, they should be allowed to exercise their role as wives and mothers." The speech centered around the need for women to receive the best education in order to enable them to develop their own qualities, escape their traditional constrictions and therefore live "content within the limits prescribed by nature."[93] In this way, he strove for a mi-way point between total ignorance and what was known as a *docta-hombruna* (literally, a learned-masculine woman),[94] advocating a woman who, while limited by her own nature, was nevertheless more than old archetypes would allow. The speech given by José María Aguirre Ortés de Velasco ascribed gender differences to novel naturalist conceptions inherent to Enlightenment thinking—to achieve the purpose, develop his gifts, the Marquis proposed a "perfect civic and political education" based on content such as the Spanish language, grammar, geography, history, French, drawing and arithmetic, singing, dancing or music.[95]

Firm in its ideas and faced with the failure of "its" *Enseñanza*, the RSBAP designed its own project, the Seminary or House of Education for Young Ladies of Vitoria, established in 1783. Conceived to complement the aims of the Patriotic Seminary of Bergara, which only admitted males, the Álavan members of the RSBAP designed a seminary for the daughters of the country's most prosperous families. There seems to be a certain degree of consensus among experts who have studied this question regarding the reason that prompted the Society to pursue the project: the impossibility of founding a seminary that was in line with their ideas in Bergara.[96]

The idea was brought to fruition by Samaniego, who by that time had already served as the director of the Patriotic Seminary of Bergara on two occasions and had published his first book of fables.[97] Finding himself at the Royal Court as a commissioner for the RSBAP, he presented the plan, which was favorably received by the Crown, as acknowledged by Minister Floridablanca in a letter sent to the Count of Peñaflorida.[98]

The RSBAP's grand plan to educate the daughters of elite families (i.e., their own daughters) was consistent with the Enlightened and utilitarian thinking that had been advocated by its members for the past two decades.[99] Thus the plans of members such as Montehermoso and Pablo de Olavide found new soil in which to flourish. As one of the seminary's staunchest advocates, the fabulist Samaniego would almost definitely had firsthand knowledge of the report written by Olavide when, as a young man, he lived with his uncle, the Count of Peñaflorida. Young Samaniego's hostility toward "nunnish" education would have been further exacerbated by the experience of his own sister, who was educated in Tudela. All this served to spur on a project that was inspired also by the institution that Catherine the Great had just created for the daughters of Russian nobles.

The Smolnyi Institute, established in 1764 in Saint Petersburg, emerged as a model for the Europe of the Enlightenment.[100] The daughters of the Russian nobility spent twelve years as boarders learning subjects such as religion, Russian and foreign languages, arithmetic, geography, history, music, dancing, drawing, home economics and domestic duties.[101] This institution would influence the development of the Basque institute, a project that was almost identical (barring certain nuances) to that designed by the Russian Empress.

The seminary was established to accept anyone who could afford it (a baptismal certificate being the only document required[102]), a stipulation included also in the statutes presented to the Crown but one which the members of the RSBAP had no intention of respecting. A secret instruction reveals that although on paper the institution was to appear inclusive, the Board of Directors (made up of members of the RSBAP) reserved the right to refuse admission, thereby guaranteeing access only to members of the nobility. In their review of the statutes, the members from Vizcaya requested that "this reserved instruction should not form part of the Code [...] it should be as follows, with the reserved instruction being the place where the Board of Directors should outline the noble qualities that must be present in the families of those aspiring to receive an education at the Seminary."[103]

Divided into groups and living as boarders, pupils received an advanced education. The youngest girls, aged between 6 and 9 years, learned to read, write and knit and studied Christian doctrine and the basics of dance. The next group, comprising those aged between 9 and 12 years, continued with their studies of religion, reading and writing, and also learned calculus, Spanish spelling and grammar, basic French, sewing, dancing, music and a little drawing. Finally, those aged between twelve and sixteen received an education focused on religious history, Spanish history, basic geography, manual skills, music, dancing, Spanish spelling and grammar, French, drawing and how to run a household—all under the supervision of the Board and the directorship of a female director with the required qualities. The faculty and other staff at the school included secular teachers, nurses, maids, a salaried priest, a bursar teacher, cooks, a porter, a purveyor, washerwomen, a physician and a surgeon.[104]

In its preamble, the RSBAP expounded on the virtues of this new type of women's education, this model that, with some nuances, was becoming steadily more popular among the Enlightened European elite of the seventeen-hundreds. According to its members, the defense of the integration of women into the political and social system through their position within the household and their right to enjoy "the delights of domestic life" justified this standard of education, which was so necessary to mold the behavior of men, who enjoyed undignified pursuits, completely lacking in nobility, such as fighting animals or governing a pack of mules. These examples were eliminated from the first plan at the recommendation of the Biscayan friends, who reasoned that said argument, the idleness of the Spanish nobility, could be used by foreign nations as a new argument against Spain.[105]

The project's ultimate aim, namely to "bring up young ladies in the utmost state of Christianity and virtue, although not for one particular state, but rather teaching them the skills appropriate for women who are destined to live nobly without the need to earn their keep with their hands," was also accompanied by a secondary one: to train "good mothers, wives and homemakers," since "women, by consent and general acceptance, are in a position to demand gifts from men in the form of civil treatment, participate with them in the care and delights of domestic life, and to have a great influence in major revolutions and political events." It was a convincing argument in favor of ensuring the moral education of women who were destined to live in a civilized world governed by androcentric and patriarchal criteria.[106]

The project formed part of a broader historical process linked to the education and significance of women, a debate that was rooted in many different concerns, such as existing deficits in their education, the reconstruction of gender roles within the family order and the emergence of different affective customs. The plan promoted by the Álavan members of the RSBAP represented this desire to orient girls' instruction toward a greater depth of knowledge. It was not a revolutionary school, nor was it the "first feminist undertaking in Spain"[107] as one author claims; rather, it was simply the brainchild of the reformist elite.

This elitist education therefore served the interests of the members' most immediate social circle. Instruction was oriented toward ensuring women were prepared to perform their role as good mothers, wives and daughters, and to redirect a view of education that stemmed from Enlightened utilitarianism.[108] Despite everything, the ladies who received an education that was so privileged yet at the same time so coerced, ended up on a novel intellectual and affective plane, during a period in which women's identity was beginning to be signified anew .

From mothers concerned about the well-being of their family and their role as wives at the beginning of the century, this new generation of women had broader horizons, more knowledge and a different kind of identity. With the arrival of Enlightenment culture, some of these families were exposed to treatises focusing on children's education and family virtuosity, works which, later on, helped them expand their perceptions, mentality and culture. Some notable (albeit rather disperse) examples include the establishment of private libraries in Vitoria,[109] Bilbao,[110] Guipúzcoa[111] and Navarra.[112] For instance, the Urbina and Gortázar families, both with connections to the RSBAP, had all kinds of books in their private libraries (see Appendix: Tables 7, 8, and 9).

The end of the eighteenth century saw the emergence of discourses on the complementarity between the sexes,[113] along with those focused on the intellectual, physical and moral differences between men and women, and those that used scientific ("biologistic") arguments to deny citizenship to women and justify their subordination.[114] They would never be citizens because they were mothers and wives,[115] something that Mary Wollstonecraft pointed out in her denunciation of the denial of women's rights based on their "different moral and physical nature."[116] Nevertheless, most of these discourses adopted a constructive and reformist approach, imbuing this new female role with public usefulness and political virtuosity. In their role as mothers, destined to educate future exemplary citizens, women found a new existential dimension[117]: "The important social-political and public function assigned to motherhood added an innovative role to the idea of the mother-educator."[118]

Another aspect worth highlighting is the sociability developed in spaces such as salons or intellectual gatherings. Eighteenth-century salons can be understood as spaces for women's learning, where they were able to participate and train to engage in public debate.[119] Here, the new habits and customs, new fads and fervor for refined manners,[120] singing and music, played a key role, all inspired by fine sentiments.[121] The Basque provinces also witnessed this *mise-en-scène* of mixed sociability, "an essential practice in modern societies that tempers customs and refines the sentiments, serving as a civilizing element."[122] In intellectual gatherings organized all over the country, women from high society demonstrated their mastery.[123]

Another important vehicle for dissemination was literature, particularly novels.[124] The evident interest in writing oriented toward women's education[125] was joined, from 1790 onward, by a sentimental fashion that extended to works of fiction also.[126] "In this eighteenth century literature, love was portrayed as a civilizing mechanism, an integrating force of everything social [...] also implicit was a reformulation of the female identity and relations between the sexes, through the re-imagining of the model of 'domestic femininity.'"[127] "The social importance of sentiments as the basic social framework for behavior"[128] was more than evident during this period.

The Enlightened discourses of the period portrayed a female figure gifted with a superior moral nature and privileged in her capacity to feel.[129] The French writer Thomas viewed female reason and sensibility on the basis of difference, seeing these qualities as evidence of women's weakness and distinct social condition: if love was the passion that women experienced best, "it is to this love that we owe their ability to entirely forget themselves and give themselves over, wholeheartedly, to others."[130] Consequently, "among women, conjugal and maternal love emerges as a natural vocation."[131] "Guided by their nature, they distance themselves from passion and are more inclined toward the ordered love of conjugal life,"[132] serving as the greatest producers of sentiments and the protagonists of family life.[133] Thanks to their innate capacity, women were given more responsibility for maintaining decency,[134] hence their importance in social interactions and their role as mothers-educators.

In the Basque Country, the speech given by the Marquis of Montehermoso during the opening ceremony of the RSBAP can be viewed as a landmark moment. His argument was based on "the inequality of the sexes, from which the different social function of each can be deduced," and raised women up in their role as "wives and mothers."[135] The Marquis praised the role of "a good Mother, an excellent *Ama*," freed from all labors that required physical strength or reflection, and criticized all external feminine attributes that were even remotely connected with luxury, superficiality or reserve—*ama* means mother in Basque, although it may also be used in the sense of owner in Spanish.[136]

In this way, key elements within the RSBAP demonstrated their commitment to defending the domestic femininity model linked to that other ideal of the complementarity between the sexes.[137] Olavide advocated "training women in spirit and heart [...] in all the virtues that a Daughter, a Wife, a Mother and a Lady should possess."[138] The importance attached to molding women's hearts and feelings is evident and the inspiration for the RSBAP Seminary stems from this idea. To train "good mothers, wives and homemakers" it was necessary to:

teach them to distinguish in all things between good and bad, the frivolous and the solid, making them see that the behavior of respected people of their sex differs only from that of those who are despised in the fact that the former choose to walk the path of goodness, of solidity.[139]

Women were therefore attributed with a prominent calling to spread civility and enjoy the delights of domestic life and political influence.[140] Their exquisite qualities were expected to influence men, thereby continuing with one of the central themes developed by the literature of the period, namely woman's "beneficial influence on man, channeling their excess passions and turning them into responsible subjects in terms of their public and private obligations."[141] Their importance in "educating male sentiment in order to construct a civilized society[142]" is evident in the preamble of the Vitoria-based project, which refers to the indignity and idleness of male nobles,[143] a stance obviously influenced by Olavide's writings.[144]

This solid moral education included a great deal of affective training in the hope of fostering calm maternal love, chastity and emotional gentleness. To this end, if they misstepped, young girls were exposed to public shame and embarrassment.[145] Taking other people, the external world, as a reference, shame was manifested as "the consequence of being sensitive to others,"[146] of complying with social expectations. Domesticated femininity was therefore a paradigm that linked the ability to be sensitive to the female gender—in the nineteenth century, emotions will be relegated to the female intimate sphere.[147]

The RSBAP project also had its limits. Women's education played a key role in the desire to improve the well-being of the Nation through its most prosperous families, those that set the tone for the Century.[148] In contrast, the Society's social impenetrability and elitism were evident in its desire to exclude all those without noble blood.[149]

But what finally happened with the project? The dream never actually came to fruition due to lack of funds and the apparent "apathy" shown by its promoters, who during that period were occupied with the management of the male school in Bergara, which by that time had the highest number of pupils in its history. The administrative obstacles to its establishment and the need to raise large sums of money may have contributed to this lack of drive shown in relation to the foundation of the Patriotic Seminary. Furthermore, the fact that those Basque settled in Mexico had their own institution, on which they were focusing all their efforts, most likely had an impact also,[150] and the subsequent French invasion, which plunged the Crown's territories in the north into an exceptional situation of total crisis, probably did not help matters either.

Despite everything, Peñaflorida never really gave up hope. In the summer of 1784, by now in a fairly delicate state of health, the Count wrote of his last and most audacious plan yet: to take over the Company of Mary's institute in Bergara. "It would be necessary to find a suitable right-hand man in Tudela to proceed with all reserve and secrecy."[151]

From here on, Munibe and his friend Álava came up with a strategy to convince Magdalena de Goizueta, an undertaking in which they involved all their fellow members and allies.[152] A classist and a breaker of conventions in equal measure, Peñaflorida aspired to building a school to protect the daughters of the region's most distinguished families from the veil. At the same time, he proposed a solution to the social problem stemming from the dowry system (see Appendix 5).

Emulating the actions of groups located in other European countries, the proposal centered on the possibility of funding "communities of Ladies who were not Nuns, such as those often seen in the Netherlands and Germany."[153] In other words, a secular institution designed to protect girls from convent life. This imagined European-style community of ladies promised to provide a distinguished educational environment in keeping with the vision held by the Society's members and far removed from the religious institutions they seemed to despise so much. It was to be a lay, autonomous and feminine space incorporated into the RSBAP.

The second daughters of noble Basque families would therefore have a dignified solution to their social situation, since as Munibe observed, many sensitive parents watched with sadness as their daughters advanced in age "without hope of improving their situation, and no choice but to become enslaved to sisters-in-law or step mothers, and to live with the sad and contemptible character of Old Girls or Ugly Women [...] the worst misfortune that can befall a Woman is to have been born into the guild of Nobility."[154] In the Basque language, a spinster was often stigmatized with the nickname *neskazahar*, literally "old girl or woman," a term similar in meaning and connotation to "old maid."

For a clear example of these disadvantages, one has to look no further than the Urbina family, one of the noble lines connected to the RSBAP.[155] The problem stemming from the large dowries required for their daughters was linked to the instrumental use of marriage, which was a strategy employed by the most prominent lineages to remain at the top of the social hierarchy.[156] It was a meditated family decision designed to respond to specific needs and which could represent a wide range of different interests, depending on the case.[157] One of the effects of this policy was the pressure put on noble lineages by the need to find dowries for their daughters, prompting many parents to deny them the right to marry (see Appendix: Table 6).[158]

In light of this situation,[159] Munibe imagined a community that would enable women to live dignified lives while waiting to marry, which they would be able to do thanks to dowries in the form of pious works offered by the institution itself. Aware that this idea was likely to be met with rejection in the region, and conscious also of the huge expense involved, the Count dreamed of convincing Magdalena: "This is my dream: and as I am accustomed to seeing other, less plausible ones of ours come to fruition, I am reluctant to keep it inside my Body; even if it generates no other effect than to divert you with its reading."[160] After a life of achievements and on the verge of catching the disease that would finally prove his downfall, this was the last great dream of the Count of Peñaflorida, first director of the RSBAP.[161]

NOTES

1 José Antonio Azpiazu Elorza, "Las escuelas en el País Vasco a principios de la Edad Moderna. El interés por la enseñanza por parte de las instituciones y particulares," *Vasconia* 27, (1998): 147-164; Francisco Javier Laspalas Pérez, "La legislación sobre escuelas de primeras letras y su administración en Navarra durante la segunda mitad del siglo XVIII," *Educación XXI* 5 (2002): 199-205; Rafael López Atxurra, "Historia de las instituciones educativas en Euskal Herria. La enseñanza primaria en el Antiguo Régimen. Pautas para la investigación," in *Haciendo Historia. Homenaje a Mª Ángeles Larrea*, ed. Rafael Mieza and Juan Gracia (Bilbao: UPV/EHU, 2004), 419-425.

2 López Atxurra, "Historia," 426-429.

3 Ibid., 433.

4 Ibid., 430. Buenaventura Delgado Criado, Historia de la educación en España y América. La educación en la España Moderna (siglos XVI-XVIII) (Madrid: Fundación Santa María, 1993), 490-497.

5   Urra Olazabal, *La educación*, 34. Según el censo de Godoy de 1801, el Reino de Navarra contaría con 300 escuelas de niños y 50 de niñas. Laspalas Pérez, "La legislación," 208.
6   Ofelia Rey Castelao, "Las experiencias cotidianas de la lectura y la escritura en el ámbito femenino," in *Vida cotidiana en la España de la Ilustración*, ed. Inmaculada Arias de Saavedra (Granada: Universidad de Granada, 2012), 616-617.
7   Urra Olazabal, *La educación*, 19-75. Jesús de Benito Pascual, *Mujer e instrucción pública. Origen del magisterio femenino en Guipúzcoa (1800-1833)* (Donostia: Gipuzkoako Foru Aldundia, Emakunde, 1999).
8   Arturo Rafael Ortega Berruguete, "Matrimonio, fecundidad y familia en el País Vasco a fines de la Edad Moderna," *Revista de Demografía Histórica* 7-1 (1989): 47-74; Jesús Turiso Sebastián, "Entre el matrimonio y el celibato. Opciones vitales de la mujer de la élite limeña del siglo XVIII," in *VIII Congreso Internacional de Historia de América*, ed. Francisco Morales Padrón (Gran Canaria: Cabildo de Gran Canaria, 2000), 1364-1379; Lola Valverde Lamsfús, "La influencia del sistema de transmisión de la herencia sobre la condición de las mujeres en el País Vasco en la Edad Moderna," *Bilduma* 5 (1991): 123-135.
9   The idea is inspired by Pilar Pérez-Fuentes Hernández, *"Ganadores de pan" y "amas de casa." Otra mirada sobre la industrialización vasca* (Bilbao: UPV/EHU, 2004).
10 José Ignacio Andrés Ucendo, "El trabajo femenino en el Bilbao de 1824," in *Historia de la mujer e historia del matrimonio*, ed. María Victoria López-Cordón and Montserrat Carbonell Esteller (Murcia: Universidad de Murcia, 1997), 317-326; Cristina Borderías, "El trabajo de las mujeres. Discursos y prácticas," in *Historia de las mujeres en España y América Latina*, ed. Isabel Morant (Madrid: Cátedra, Volume 3, 2005), 353-380; Nicole Pellegrin, "Las costureras de la historia: mujeres y trabajo en el Antiguo Régimen. Un balance historiográfico," *Arenal* 1-1 (1994): 25-38; Francisco Ramiro Moya, *Mujeres y trabajo en la Zaragoza del siglo XVIII* (Zaragoza: Prensas universitarias de Zaragoza, 2012); Ofelia Rey Castelao, "El trabajo de las mujeres rurales en la España moderna: un balance historiográfico (1994-2013)," *Revista de historiografía* 23-1 (2015): 183-210.
11 María Rosario Roquero Ussía, "El convento y la política matrimonial de la burguesía donostiarra," *Boletín de Estudios Históricos de San Sebastián* 47 (2014): 129-133; Fernanda Prada Camín, *Ocho siglos de historia de las clarisas en España* (Murcia: Editorial Espigas, 2013); Nere Jone Intxaustegi Jauregi, *La mujer religiosa en Bizkaia durante los siglos XVI-XVIII* (Bilbao: Diputación Foral de Bizkaia, 2018).
12 Barrio Moya, "La librería," 165.
13 Paloma Manzanos Arreal and Francisca Vives Casas, *Las mujeres en Vitoria-Gasteiz a lo largo de los siglos. Recorridos y biografías* (Vitoria-Gasteiz: Ayuntamiento de Vitoria-Gasteiz, 2001), 28-29.
14 Ofelia Rey Castelao, "Libros y lecturas en la España de Carlos II," *E-Spania. Revue interdisciplinaire d'etudes hispaniques médiévales et modernes* 29 (2018).
15 Urra Olazabal, *La Compañía*, 40.
16 Urra Olazabal, *La educación*, 96.
17 Ibid., 98-99; Urra Olazabal, *La Compañía*, 40.
18 Urra Olazabal, *La educación*, 99-100.
19 Mª Rosa Ayerbe Iribar, "Manuel de Larramendi y la enseñanza femenina en el siglo XVIII. Constituciones del Seminario de niñas "Nuestra Señora de la Soledad," de Bergara (1741)," *Boletín de la RSBAP* 64-2 (2008): 797-801. For an approach to the Jesuit's vision

of Gipuzkoan femininity, Bakarne Altonaga, "Mujeres viriles en el siglo XVIII. La construcción de la feminidad por el discurso foralista de Manuel de Larramendi," *Historia Contemporánea* 52 (2016): 9-42.
20   Ibid., 797-801. Luis Enrique Rodriguez-San Pedro Bezares, *Sensibilidades religiosas del Barroco: Carmelitas descalzas en San Sebastián* (San Sebastián: Kutxa, 1990); Luis Enrique Rodriguez-San Pedro Bezares, "Claustros femeninos en la Ilustración: las carmelitas descalzas de San Sebastián," *Boletín de la RSBAP* 64-2 (2008): 771-794.
21   Ibid., 799.
22   Ibid., 799-808. For an approach to the linguistic situation of the Basque territories in the Modern Age, Juan Madariaga Orbea, *Sociedad y lengua vasca en los siglos XVII y XVIII* (Bilbao: Eukaltzaindia, 2014).
23   Ibid., 812. Urra Olazabal, *La educación*, 100. Gabriela Vives Almandoz, "La correspondencia de Miguel José de Olaso Zumalabe (1718-1773), primer secretario perpetuo de la Real Sociedad Bascongada de los Amigos del País," in *II Seminario de Historia de la RSBP* (Donostia: RSBAP, 1988), 197-220.
24   Urra Olazabal, *La educación*, 106-107; Urra Olazabal, *La Compañía*, 40-46.
25   Urra Olazabal, *La educación*, 108-114.
26   Alejandro Cardozo Uzcátegui, "El lobby cisatlántico del cacao. La Real Compañía Guipuzcoana de Caracas y el poder vasco en la provincia de Venezuela," in *Recuperando el Norte. Empresas, capitales y proyectos atlánticos en la economía imperial hispánica*, ed. Alberto Angulo Morales and Álvaro Aragón Ruano (Bilbao: UPV/EHU, 2016), 195-216; Ricardo Cierbide Martinena, "La Compañía Guipuzcoana de Caracas y los vascos en Venezuela durante el siglo XVIII," *Revista Internacional de Estudios Vascos* 42-1 (1997): 63-75; Irene Fattaccia, "The Resilience and Boomerang Effect of Chocolate: A Product's Globalization and Commodification," in *Global Goods and the Spanish Empire, 1492-1824. Circulation, Resistance and Diversity*, ed. Bethany Aram and Bartolomé Yun-Casalilla, Bartolomé (London: Palgrave Macmillan, 2014), 255-273; Montserrat Gárate Ojanguren, "Las cuentas de la Real Compañía Guipuzcoana de Caracas," *Moneda y Crédito* 153 (1980): 49-75; Montserrat Gárate Ojanguren, *La Real Compañía Guipuzcoana de Caracas* (San Sebastián: Sociedad Guipuzcoana de Ediciones y Publicaciones, 1990), 519-584; José Garmendia Arruebarrena, "La Real Compañía Guipuzcoana de Caracas y su contribución en Sevilla," *Cuadernos de Sección, Eusko Ikaskuntza, Sociedad de Estudios Vascos* 8 (1986): 48-58; *Los vascos y América. Actas de las Jornadas sobre el comercio vasco con América en el siglo XVIII y la Real Compañía Guipuzcoana de Caracas en el II centenario de Carlos II* (Bilbao: Fundación Banco de Vizcaya, 1980); Adelina Rodríguez Mirabal, "La España reformista de comienzos del siglo XVIII y la nueva orientación del comercio ultramarino (El caso de la Compañía Guipuzcoana de Caracas)," *Ensayos Históricos. Anuario del Instituto de Estudios Hispánicos* 13 (2001): 39-54; Gerardo Vivas Pineda, *La aventura naval de la Compañía Guipuzcoana de Caracas* (Caracas: Fundación Polar, 1998); Gerardo Vivas Pineda, "La Compañía Guipuzcoana de Caracas: los buques y sus hombres," in *Los vascos y América. Actas de las Jornadas sobre el comercio vasco con América en el siglo XVIII y la Real Compañía Guipuzcoana de Caracas en el II centenario de Carlos II* (Bilbao: Fundación Banco de Vizcaya, 1980), 313-317.
27   Urra Olazabal, *La educación*, 127-129.
28   Ibid., 130.

29 Gárate Ojanguren, *La Real Compañía*, 348.
30 For an analysis of the Goizuetas and their links with the RCGC, Vicente de Amezaga, *Hombres de la Compañía Guipuzcoana* (Bilbao: Editorial La Gran Enciclopedia Vasca, Volume II, 1979), 93 and 242-245; Arantzazu Amezaga Iribarren, "La Real Compañía Guipuzcoana de Caracas. Crónica sentimental con una visión historiográfica. Los años áuricos y las rebeliones (1728-1751)," *Sancho el Sabio. Revista de cultura e investigación vasca* 23 (2005): 167-208; Montserrat Gárate Ojanguren, "Navarros y guipuzcoanos unidos en empresas económicas del siglo XVIII," *Revista Internacional de Estudios Vascos* 37-1 (1992): 25-42; Urra Olazabal, *La educación*, 127-134.
31 Urra Olazabal, *La Compañía*, 52; Urra Olazabal, *La educación*, 146.
32 Urra Olazabal, *La educación*, 147.
33 Elena Alcorta Ortiz de Zárate, "La importancia del comercio en el siglo XVIII y su influencia en la RSBAP," in *Ilustración, ilustraciones*, ed. Jesús Astigarraga Goenaga, María Victoria López-Cordón Cortezo and José María Urquía Echave (Madrid: Sociedad Estatal de Conmemoraciones Culturales, Volume 2, 2009), 953-966.
34 Muriel, "La sociedad novohispana," 277.
35 Ángela Atienza López, " 'No pueden ellos ver mejor. . . .' Autonomía, autoridad y sororidad en el gobierno de los claustros femeninos en la Edad Moderna," *Arenal* 26-1 (2019): 5-34.
36 The role as administrator of Miguel José de Olaso y Zumalabe can be seen through his private correspondence. As an example, letter from Ignacio Antonio de Lopeola to Miguel José de Olaso y Zumalabe, San Sebastian, 07/31/1770. Archivo de la Casa Zavala [ACZ], Correspondencia de la Casa de Olaso, 242.2.
37 Urra Olazabal, *La educación*, 145.
38 Álvaro Chaparro Sainz, "Del pupitre a la espada: el Real Seminario de Vergara, cantera de militares," *Revista de Demografía Histórica* 27 (2009): 64.
39 Francisco Aguilar Piñal, Bibliografía de la Real Sociedad Vascongada de los Amigos del País en el siglo XVIII (San Sebastián: CSIC (1971).
40 Astigarraga, "Sociedades," 677-679.
41 Ibid., 150-151.
42 Archivo del Territorio Histórico de Álava [ATHA], Fondo Prestamero, caja 8, Nº 16.1.
43 Letter from Xavier María de Munibe to Pedro Jacinto de Álava, Bergara, 01/06/1775. In José Ignacio Tellechea Idígoras, *La Ilustración vasca. Cartas de Xabier de Munibe, Conde de Peñaflorida, a Pedro Jacinto de Álava* (Vitoria-Gasteiz: Eusko Legebiltzarra-Parlamento Vasco, 1987), 294-295. For an approach to the rich correspondence between both characters, Cécile Mary Trojani, "Aproximación semántica a un epistolario. Los tratamientos en la correspondencia entre Peñaflorida y Pedro Jacinto de Álava," in *La carta como fuente y como texto. Las correspondencias societarias del siglo XVIII: La Real Sociedad Bascongada de los Amigos del País*, ed. José María Urquía Echave and Antonio Risco (Donostia: RSBAP, 2005), 239-254; Cécile Mary Trojani, "La amistad en el Siglo de las Luces. La Real Sociedad Bascongada en las fuentes epistolares," *Boletín de la RSBAP* 60-2 (2004): 609-628.
44 ATHA, Fondo Prestamero, caja 8, Nº 16.3. También analizado en Urra Olazabal, *La educación*, 170-171.
45 ATHA, Fondo Prestamero, caja 8, Nº 16.3.
46 Letter from Xabier María de Munibe to Pedro Jacinto de Álava, Bergara, 02/17/1775. Tellechea Idígoras, *La Ilustración vasca*, 313.

47 Recarte Barriola, *Ilustración vasca*, 120.
48 Archivo del Parlamento Vasco [APV], Fondo Álava, legajo 3.
49 ATHA, Fondo Prestamero, caja 8, N° 16.5.
50 Letter from Pedro Jacinto de Álava to Pablo de Olavide, Vitoria, 09/01/1774. ATHA, Fondo Prestamero, caja 31, N° 70.
51 For an approach to Pablo de Olavide, María José Alonso Seoane, "El último sueño de Pablo de Olavide," *Cuadernos Dieciochistas* 4 (2003): 47-65; Luis Perdices de Blas, *Pablo de Olavide (1725-1803), el ilustrado* (Madrid: Universidad Complutense, 1993); Antonio Viñao Frago, "La influencia de Campomanes, Olavide y Cabarrús en la educación," in *Historia de la educación en España y América*, ed. Buenaventura Delgado Criado (Madrid: Morata, Volume II, 1993), 657-668.
52 Luis Perdices de Blas, "Mujer, educación y mercado de trabajo en el proyecto reformista de Pablo de Olavide," *ICE: Revista de Economía* 852 (2010): 99-111.
53 Archivo Municipal de Bergara [AMB], 03-C/123-006.
54 AMB, 03-C/123-006.
55 AMB, 03-C/123-006.
56 AMB, 03-C/123-006.
57 AMB, 03-C/123-006.
58 Letter from Pablo de Olavide to Pedro Jacinto de Álava, Seville, 02/13/1775. AMB, 03-C/123-006.
59 Letter from Xabier María de Munibe to Pedro Jacinto de Álava, Bergara, 03/28/1775. Tellechea Idígoras, *La Ilustración vasca*, 330. Letter from Xabier María de Munibe to Pedro Jacinto de Álava, Bergara, 02/27/1775. Tellechea Idígoras, *La Ilustración vasca*, 317. Letter from Xabier María de Munibe to Pedro Jacinto de Álava, Bergara, 03/10/1775. Ibid., 320. Perdices de Blas, "Mujer, educación," 108.
60 Letter from Xabier María de Munibe to Pedro Jacinto de Álava, Bergara, 03/11/1775. Ibid., 321.
61 Letter from Xabier María de Munibe to Pedro Jacinto de Álava, Bergara, 03/19/1775. Ibid., 325.
62 Bergara, 04/03/1775. ATHA, Fondo Prestamero, caja 8, N° 16.6.
63 Bergara, 07/03/1775. ATHA, Fondo Prestamero, caja 8, N° 16.6.
64 ATHA, Fondo Prestamero, caja 8, N° 16.6.
65 ATHA, Fondo Prestamero, caja 8, N° 16.6.
66 ATHA, Fondo Prestamero, caja 8, N° 16.6.
67 Vitoria, 04/06/1775. ATHA, Fondo Prestamero, caja 8, N° 16.6.
68 Bergara, 04/07/1775. ATHA, Fondo Prestamero, caja 8, N° 16.5.
69 Tellechea Idígoras, *La Ilustración vasca*, 255.
70 ATHA, Fondo Prestamero, caja 8, N° 16.5. Studies that have addressed the issue of reports can be found in Emilio Palacios Fernández, *La mujer y las letras en la España del siglo XVIII* (Madrid: Laberinto, 2002), 78-82; Recarte Barriola, *Ilustración vasca*, 116-124; Urra Olazabal, *La educación*, 150-179; Urra Olazabal, *La Compañía*, 84-88.
71 Maite Recarte Barriola, "La renovación educativa de la Ilustración vasca: la Real Sociedad Bascongada de los Amigos del País," *Revista Internacional de los Estudios Vascos* 37-2 (1992): 321.
72 Emilio Palacios Fernández, "Samaniego y la educación en la Sociedad Bascongada de Amigos del País," in *I Seminario de historia de la Real Sociedad Bascongada de los Amigos*

del País (San Sebastián: RSBAP, 1986), 288. *Auñamendi Eusko Entziklopedia* (Eusko Ikaskuntza) [consulted by el 02/10/2017].
73 Recarte Barriola, *Ilustración vasca*, 122 y 148-150.
74 Letter from the Viscount of Ambite to the Count of Peñaflorida, Vitoria, 08/20/1767. ATHA, Fondo Prestamero, caja 32, Nº 3.
75 Urra Olazabal, *La educación*, 178.
76 ATHA, Fondo Prestamero, caja 8, Nº 16.5.
77 Letter from Pedro Jacinto de Álava to Xabier María de Munibe, Madrid, 03/03/1774. ATHA, Fondo Prestamero, caja 31, Nº 138.
78 Letter from Pedro Jacinto de Álava to Xabier María de Munibe, Madrid, 03/07/1774. ATHA, Fondo Prestamero, caja 31, Nº 139.
79 Letter from Pedro Jacinto de Álava to Xabier María de Munibe, Madrid, 03/10/1774. ATHA, Fondo Prestamero, caja 31, Nº 140. The swap negotiations dragged on for weeks. ATHA, Fondo Prestamero, caja 31, Nº 141 and 146.
80 Letters from Pedro Jacinto de Álava to Xabier María de Munibe, Vitoria, 01/22/1775 and 01/26/1775. ATHA, Fondo Prestamero, caja 31, Nº 167 y 168. Tellechea Idígoras, *La Ilustración vasca*, 298-307.
81 Letter from the Marquis of Valdelirios to Xabier María de Munibe, Madrid, 07/03/1775. ATHA, Fondo Prestamero, caja 36, Nº 138. Juan Luis Blanco Mozo, *Orígenes y desarrollo de la Ilustración vasca en Madrid. De la Congregación de San Ignacio a la Sociedad Bascongada* (Madrid: Real Sociedad Bascongada de los Amigos del País, 2011).
82 Recarte Barriola, *Ilustración vasca*, 218.
83 Ester Barberá Heredia, "Perspectiva socio-cognitiva: estereotipos y esquemas de género," in *Psicología y género*, ed. Ester Barberá and Isabel Martínez Benlloch (Madrid: Pearson Prentice Hall, 2004), 58-69.
84 Urra Olazabal, *La Compañía*, 52 and 96.
85 Letter from Xabier María de Munibe to Pedro Jacinto de Álava, Logroño, 06/25/1784. APV, Fondo Álava, legajo 3.
86 Ibid.
87 María Teresa Gabarain, "La influencia europea en la Ilustración del País Vasco. Presencia de jóvenes vascos en los colegios franceses durante el siglo XVIII," in *V Seminario de Historia de la RSBAP* (Donostia-San Sebastián: RSBAP, 1996), 750.
88 Recarte Barriola, *Ilustración vasca*, 123-124. The complete letter from Gaspar de Munibe to his nephew can be found in *Colección de documentos inéditos para la historia de Guipúzcoa* (San Sebastián: Diputación de Guipúzcoa, 1965), 25.
89 Gabarain, "La influencia," 743-754.
90 Urra Olazabal, *La educación*, 90.
91 Maite Recarte Barriola, "Ideario pedagógico de la Real Sociedad Bascongada de los Amigos del País, según los discursos de sus Juntas Generales," in *I Seminario de historia de la Real Sociedad Bascongada de los Amigos del País* (San Sebastián: RSBAP, 1986), 319.
92 Xabier María de Munibe, "Historia de la Real Sociedad Bascongada," *Revista Internacional de Estudios Vascos* 22 (1931): 450-453.
93 Palacios Fernández, *La mujer*, 76-77. "Education, however, alters the attributes with which nature enriched this sex, and that which in the first state had an incontestable power, loses it with its rich gifts due to an unhappy upbringing." Munibe, "Historia," 451.

94 Recarte Barriola, "Ideario pedagógico," 320. "The one that the woman plays the learned, makes her lose the most beautiful of her graces; but this does not mean that she has to be condemned to the center of ignorance, and to the need to remain silent or to be unable to speak except about uselessness or even worse things, such as gossip." Munibe, "Historia," 452.
95 Palacios Fernández, *La mujer*, 76-77; Recarte Barriola, *Ilustración vasca*, 113-114; Recarte Barriola, "Ideario pedagógico," 319-320.
96 Urra Olazabal, *La Compañía*, 94. In a later work, he attributes it to the delay in opening the Teaching and the rejection of his pedagogical ideas. Recarte Barriola, *Ilustración vasca*, 125; Miren Sánchez Erauskin, "Plan y ordenanzas de un seminario o casa de educación de señoritas. El proyecto de la Real Sociedad Bascongada de los Amigos del País," in *I Seminario de historia de la Real Sociedad Bascongada de los Amigos del País* (San Sebastián: RSBAP, 1986), 326; Urra Olazabal, *La educación*, 117.
97 Palacios Fernández, "Samaniego," 296-297.
98 ATHA, Fondo Prestamero, caja 8, Nº 18. We also find the full transcript at Palacios Fernández, "Samaniego," 308.
99 Mónica Bolufer Peruga, Arte y artificio de la vida en común. Los modelos de comportamiento y sus tensiones en el siglo de las Luces (Madrid: Marcial Pons, 2019), 213.
100 Carolyn C. Lougee, ""Its Frequent Visitor." Death at Boarding School in Early Modern Europe," in *Women's Education in Early Modern Europe. A History, 1500-1800*, ed. Barbara J. Whitehead (New York: Garland Publishing, 1999), 204.
101 Robin Bisha, Jehanne M. Gheith, Christine Holden and William G. Wagner, *Russian Women. Experience & Expression. An Anthology of Sources* (Bloomington: Indiana University Press, 2002), 163.
102 AMB, 03-C/123-006.
103 Biblioteca Nacional de España [BNE], MSS/22012/2.
104 ATHA, Fondo Prestamero, caja 8, Nº 18.
105 BNE, MSS/22012/2.
106 ATHA, Fondo Prestamero, caja 8, Nº 18.
107 José Antonio Vaca de Osma, *Los vascos en la historia de España* (Madrid: Rialp, 1995), 119.
108 Ibid., 345-414.
109 Alberto Angulo Morales, *Del éxito en los negocios al fracaso del Consulado. La formación de la burguesía mercantil de Vitoria (1670-1840)* (Bilbao: UPV/EHU, 2000), 524-539; Rosario Porres Marijuán, "Los protocolos notariales e Historia de la cultura. La biblioteca de don Diego Manuel de Esquivel y Verástegui" en *Aproximación metodológica a los protocolos notariales de Álava (Edad Moderna)*, ed. Rosario Porres Marijuán (Bilbao: UPV/EHU, 1996), 327-344.
110 Elena Alcorta Ortiz de Zárate, La burguesía mercantil en el Bilbao del siglo XVIII. Los Gómez de la Torre y Mazarredo (San Sebastián: Txertoa, 2003), 162-165.
111 Barrio Moya, "La librería"; José Luis Barrio Moya, "La biblioteca de Doña Luisa de Urrieta, dama donostiarra en el Madrid de Felipe V," *Boletín de la RSBAP* 54-2 (1998): 435-445; José Luis Barrio Moya, "La biblioteca de Doña Marcela Arteaga Arenaza y Tellechea, una dama bilbaína en el Madrid de Carlos IV (1805)," *Boletín de la RSBAP* 66-2 (2010): 639-651; Juan Madariaga Orbea and Javier Esteban Ochoa de Eribe, "Experiencias divergentes, lecturas diferenciales. Los propietarios de bibliotecas particulares de Guipúzcoa (1675-1849)," *Historia social* 89 (2017): 139-156.

112 Fernando Mikelarena Peña, "La biblioteca de un notable rural. La colección de don Francisco de Echarren y Atondo, hacendado de Valtierra," *Príncipe de Viana* 65 (2004): 917-945; Fernando Mikelarena Peña, "La biblioteca de Pedro Miguel de Ligués, comerciante de lanas de Cintruénigo," *Sancho el Sabio* 23 (2005): 63-88; Fernando Mikelarena Peña, "La cultura libraria en la Navarra rural entre 1750 y 1849," *Historia Contemporánea* 34 (2007): 283-322; Fernando Mikelarena Peña, "El final de una biblioteca centenaria. La historia de la Biblioteca de la Real Sociedad Tudelana de los Deseosos del Bien Público," *Revista Internacional de Estudios Vascos* 53-1 (2008): 183-215; Fernando Mikelarena Peña, "La biblioteca de Francisco Javier Vidarte y Mendinueta, un liberal navarro," *Bulletin Hispanique* 110-2 (2008): 449-485; Fernando Mikelarena Peña, "Los libros de historia de la biblioteca de Juan Antonio Fernández, erudito tudelano y académico correspondiente de la RAH," *Príncipe de Viana* 69 (2008): 459-495.
113 Gloria Franco Rubio, "La contribución literaria de Moratín y otros hombres de letras al modelo de mujer doméstica," *Cuadernos de Historia Moderna* 6 (2007): 252.
114 Celia Amorós Puente, "Simone de Beauvoir: entre la vindicación y la crítica al Androcentrismo," *Investigaciones Feministas* 0 (2009): 12; Elena Barbieri and Rosa de Castro, "Ciudadanía y feminismo: categorías a debatir," in *Actas de las XIII Jornadas Rosarinas de Antropología Socio-cultural* (Rosario: Universidad de Rosario, 2016), 4-7; Rosa María Capel Martínez, "Preludio de una emancipación: la emergencia de la mujer ciudadana," *Cuadernos de Historia Moderna* 6 (2007): 161-162.
115 Barbieri and Castro, "Ciudadanía and feminismo," 7.
116 Encarna Bodelón, "Feminismo y Derecho: mujeres que van más allá de lo jurídico," in *Género y dominación. Críticas feministas del derecho y el poder*, ed. Gemma Nicolás and Encarna Bodelón (Barcelona: Anthropos, 2009), 98.
117 Mónica Bolufer Peruga, "Josefa Amar e Inés Joyes: dos perspectivas femeninas sobre el matrimonio en el siglo XVIII," in *Historia de la mujer e historia del matrimonio*, ed. María Victoria López-Cordón and Montserrat Carbonell Esteller (Murcia: Universidad de Murcia, 1997), 203-217; María Victoria López-Cordón, *Condición femenina y razón ilustrada. Josefa Amar y Borbón* (Zaragoza: Universidad de Zaragoza, 2006); Constance A. Sullivan, "Las escritoras del siglo XVIII," in *Breve historia feminista de la literatura española (en lengua castellana)*, ed. Iris M. Zavala (Barcelona: Anthropos, Tomo IV, 1997), 325-330.
118 Capel Martínez, "Preludio," 172-179.
119 McClelland, *The education*, 23.
120 Robert Johnson and Maite Zubiaurre, *Antropología del pensamiento feminista español* (Madrid: Cátedra, 2012), 45-51.
121 Mónica Bolufer Peruga, "Sociabilidad mixta y civilización: miradas desde España," in *Educar los sentimientos y las costumbres. Una mirada desde la historia*, ed. Mónica Bolufer, Carolina Blutrach and Juan Gomis (Zaragoza: Institución Fernando el Católico, CSIC, 2014), 149-173; María de los Ángeles Pérez Samper, "Espacios y prácticas de sociabilidad en el siglo XVIII: tertulias, refrescos y cafés de Barcelona," *Cuadernos de Historia Moderna* 26 (2001): 11-55.
122 Bolufer Peruga, "Sociabilidad mixta," 151. See Fernando Ampudia de Haro, "Cortesía y prudencia: una gestión civilizada del comportamiento y de las emociones," in *Accidentes del alma. Las emociones en la Edad Moderna*, ed. María Tausiet and James S. Amelang (Madrid: Abada Editores, 2009), 123-143.
123 Fundación Sancho el Sabio-Caja Vital/Vital Kutxa, Archivo del Marqués de la Alameda [AMA], VELASCO, C.144, N.6; AMA, URBINA, C.25, N.5; AMA, URBINA, C.76,

N.22; María Jesús Cava Mesa, *Un paseo por la historia de Bilbao* (Bilbao: Universidad de Deusto, 2008), 98; Munibe, "Historia," 453; Urra Olazabal, *La Compañía*, 185.

124 José Jesús López Céspedes, "Novela del siglo XVIII y construcción de la sentimentalidad ilustrada en España. "Voz de la naturaleza" de I. García Malo," in *El mundo hispánico en el Siglo de las Luces* (Madrid: Universidad Complutense de Madrid, Volume 2, 1996), 831-842; Isabel Morant Deusa, "Educar deleitando. Los usos de la novela formativa en el siglo XVIII," in *El siglo XVIII en femenino. Las mujeres en el Siglo de las Luces*, ed. Manuel-Reyes García Hurtado (Madrid: Síntesis, 2016), 277-292; Isabel Morant Deusa, "Las costumbres del amor y la diferencia de sexos en la novela de la modernidad," in *Las huellas de Foucault en la historiografía. Poderes, cuerpos y deseos*, ed. Henar Gallego Franco and Isabel del Val Valdivieso (Barcelona: Icaria, 2013), 135-162; Isabel Morant Deusa and Mónica Bolufer Peruga, *Amor, matrimonio y familia. La construcción histórica de la familia moderna* (Madrid: Síntesis, 1998).

125 Bolufer Peruga, *Arte y artificio*, 208.

126 Mónica Bolufer Peruga, "Afectos razonables: equilibrios de la sensibilidad dieciochesca," in *La cultura de las emociones y las emociones en la cultura española contemporánea (siglos XVIII-XXI)*, ed. Luisa Elena Delgado, Pura Fernández and Jo Labanyi (Madrid: Cátedra, 2018), 39. To delve into the relationship between women and literature during the period, Nieves Baranda, *Cortejo a lo prohibido. Lectoras y escritoras en la España moderna* (Madrid: Arco, 2005); Rey Castelao, "Las experiencias cotidianas," 615-644.

127 María José de la Pascua Sánchez, "Una aproximación a la Historia de la familia como espacio de afectos y desafectos: el mundo hispánico del Setecientos," *Chronica Nova* 27 (2000): 136-137.

128 Rosa María Medina Doménech, "Sentir la Historia. Propuestas para una agenda de investigación feminista en la historia de las emociones," *Arenal* 19-1 (2012): 165-166.

129 Mónica Bolufer Peruga, "En torno a la sensibilidad dieciochesca: discursos, prácticas, paradojas," in *Las mujeres y las emociones en Europa y América. Siglos XVII-XIX*, ed. María Luisa Candau Chacón (Santander: Universidad de Cantabria, 2016), 35.

130 Isabel Morant Deusa, "¿Qué es una mujer? O la condición sentimental de la mujer," in *Mujeres en la historia del pensamiento*, ed. Rosa María Rodríguez Magda (Barcelona: Anthropos, 1997), 147-152.

131 Bolufer Peruga, "Afectos razonables: equilibrios," 47.

132 Morant Deusa, "¿Qué es una mujer?," 153-155.

133 Isabel Morant Deusa, "El hombre y la mujer en el matrimonio. Moral y sentimientos familiares," in *Familia y organización social en Europa y América, siglos XV-XX*, ed. Francisco Chacón Jiménez, Juan Hernández Franco and Francisco García González (Murcia: Universidad de Murcia, 2007), 204. Véase Cantero Rosales, "De "perfecta casada."

134 Mónica Bolufer Peruga, "Modelar conductas y sensibilidades: un campo abierto de indagación histórica," in *Educar los sentimientos y las costumbres. Una mirada desde la historia*, ed. Mónica Bolufer, Carolina Blutrach and Juan Gomis (Zaragoza: Institución Fernando el Católico, CSIC, 2014), 7-9.

135 Munibe, "Historia," 450-453.

136 Munibe, "Historia," 453.

137 Mónica Bolufer Peruga, "De violentar las pasiones a educar el sentimiento: el matrimonio and la civilidad Dieciochesca," in *Actas de la XI Reunión Científica de la Fundación Española de Historia Moderna* (Granada: Universidad de Granada, Volume 2, 2012), 355; Franco Rubio, "La contribución literaria," 252.

138 AMB, 03-C/123-006.
139 Copia del plan y Ordenanzas de un seminario o casa de educación para señoritas que se intenta establecer en la Ciudad de Vitoria. ATHA, 1784/03/12.
140 ATHA, Fondo Prestamero, caja 8, Nº 18.
141 Bolufer Peruga, "Afectos razonables: equilibrios," 47.
142 Ibid., 47.
143 Idea abreviada se un Seminario o Casa de educación que se intenta establecer en la Ciudad de Vitoria bajo la dirección de la R. S. B. de los Amigos del País. APV, Fondo Álava, legajo 3.
144 AMB, 03-C/123-006.
145 ATHA, 1784/03/12.
146 Ana Isabel Vergara Iraeta, "Sexo e Identidad de Género: Diferencias en el Conocimiento Social de las Emociones y en el Modo de Compartirlas" (Tesis doctoral, UPV/EHU, 1992), 247-248.
147 Luisa Elena Delgado, Pura Fernández and Jo Labanyi, "Cartografía de las emociones en la cultura española contemporánea: teorías, prácticas y contextos culturales," in *La cultura de las emociones y las emociones en la cultura española contemporánea (siglos XVIII-XXI)*, ed. Luisa Elena Delgado, Pura Fernández and Jo Labanyi (Madrid: Cátedra, 2018), 11; Bolufer Peruga, "Afectos razonables: equilibrios," 35.
148 AMB, 03-C/123-006.
149 BNE, MSS/22012/2.
150 Recarte Barriola, *Ilustración vasca*, 129.
151 Letter from Xabier María de Munibe to Pedro Jacinto de Álava, Logroño, 07/09/1784. APV, Fondo Álava, legajo 3. Tellechea Idígoras, *La Ilustración vasca*.
152 Letter from Pedro Jacinto de Álava to Xabier María de Munibe, Vitoria, 07/17/1784. ATHA, Fondo Prestamero, caja 31, Nº 192; Letter from Xavier María de Munibe to Pedro Jacinto de Álava, Logroño, 07/19/1784. APV, Fondo Álava, legajo 3; Letter from Xabier María de Munibe to Pedro Jacinto de Álava, Logroño, 07/23/1784. APV, Fondo Álava, legajo 3.
153 Letter from Xabier María de Munibe to Pedro Jacinto de Álava, Logroño, 06/25/1784. APV, Fondo Álava, legajo 3.
154 Ibid.
155 Iker Echeberria Ayllón, "Breve aproximación a la autoridad femenina en el s. XVIII. El extraño caso de Gregoria de Urbina," *Sancho el Sabio. Revista de cultura e investigación vasca* 37 (2014): 33-52.
156 Borja de Aguinagalde, *Guía para la reconstrucción de familias en Guipúzcoa (XV-XIX)* (Donostia: Gipuzkoako Foru Aldundia, 1994), 21; Jesús Arpal Poblador, *La sociedad tradicional*, 145-162 and 177-191; Jesús Turiso Sebastián, "Las claves de la armonía social. Matrimonio, patria potestad y dotes en la América virreinal," in *Dote matrimonial y redes de poder en el Antiguo Régimen en España e Hispanoamérica*, ed. Nora L. Siegrist de Gentile, and Edda O. Samudio (Mérida: Universidad de los Andes, 2006), 197-216.
157 The example of the founding families of the RSBAP is illustrative, related to each other. Borja de Aguinagalde, "La fundación de la Real Sociedad Bascongada de los Amigos del País ¿un asunto de familia?," in *II Seminario de Historia de la Real Sociedad Bascongada de Amigos del País* (Donostia-San Sebastián: RSBAP, 1988), 395-444; Álvaro Chaparro Sainz, "La política educativa de las familias ilustradas vascas. La familia Álava y el Real Seminario

de Vergara," in *Familias, jerarquización y movilidad social*, ed. Giovanni Levi and Raimundo E. Rodríguez Pérez (Murcia: Universidad de Murcia, 2010), 72-73.

158 Other examples in Angulo Morales, *De Cameros*, 63-68 and 95-113; Angulo Morales, *Del éxito*, 521-524.

159 Aguinagalde, *Guía para*, 21; Arpal Poblador, *La sociedad tradicional*, 145-162; Valverde Lamsfús, "La influencia," 123-135.

160 Letter from Xabier María de Munibe to Pedro Jacinto de Álava, Logroño, 06/25/1784. APV, Fondo Álava, legajo 3.

161 Jon Bagües i Erriondo, "El conde de Peñaflorida, impulsor de la Ilustración musical en el País Vasco," *Musiker, Cuadernos de Música* 4 (1988): 123; Tellechea Idígoras, *La Ilustración vasca*, 774-787.

CONCLUSIONS

After almost seventy years, women's education finally began to change, mainly thanks to the firm will of certain nuns, the steadfast efforts of Basques settled in New Spain, and the interests of the proreform elite. But it only changed for some; for many others it remained exactly the same.

In 1799, the Bergara *Enseñanza* (which still operates to this very day) finally opened its doors. During this period, several Basque municipalities began to open elementary schools for girls, an impulse that spread throughout the Spanish Empire following the publication of a Royal Decree by King Carlos III in 1783.[1] The Godoy Census, conducted in 1879, counted three girls' schools in Álava, eighteen in Señorío de Vizcaya and thirty-five in the province of Guipúzcoa, which together provided an education to 2,280 female students.[2] Some women were also educated at various religious institutions and others (especially the wealthiest ones) received private instruction at home.

The transformation process was not without its failures, mainly suffered in this case by the proreformist elite. The setbacks were not so much due to the innovative nature of their postulates or to a lack of good intentions, but rather to the fact that their aspirations were never actually materialized. The demise of the Count of Peñaflorida in 1785 marked the end of the Basque Enlightenment era and its dreams to educate women. The Vitoria House of Education for Young Ladies was never established and the project advocated by Magdalena de Goizueta prevailed over all others. However, although the traditional education model continued to be applied to the majority, a select few did benefit from certain changes. This was because the instrumental failure of the projects advocated by members of the Basque Enlightenment movement did not mean that the new way of viewing women's education and the female condition in general disappeared altogether, and the warmth of this transformed hearth fire continued to emanate into the world.

The long-distance analysis carried out on some houses belonging to that Basque enlightened circle demonstrates mutability. If we look at the examples of the Urbina family, the Mazarredos or the Biscayan Gortázar, we discover the process. The women belonging to these lineages gradually received a more complete training, or if you want, a more enriched one, a generational evolution that explains part of the changes experienced in terms of social treatment or development of new identities. In New Spain, the education of the most privileged classes underwent a similar process also.[3]

The bonds and relationships forged among Basques living in the Basque Country and those settled in America affected the development of women's education. From the moment they were first published, Samaniego's fables also proved vital to the education of New Spanish women—a clear example of this transatlantic cultural transfer.[4] Conversely, the success of his work was partly due at least to the influence of the Mexican members of the RSBAP.[5]

Individually and institutionally, the two territories behaved like communicating vessels. The founder of the Mexican *Enseñanza* imported the model developed by the Company of Mary in Navarra, her family's homeland. And similarly to the RSBAP Seminary, Magdalena de Goizueta brought her project to fruition thanks to money from America. Inversely, the success of the *Vizcaínas* School was largely due to the support provided by the Basque institutions. And finally, there was the advent of the Enlightenment, a movement that, thanks to preexisting structures and relationships, quickly spread throughout New Spain.

Upon analyzing the education fostered by Basques on both sides of the Atlantic, several commonalities emerge, along with various differences and a large accumulation of interests. The education model developed by the Basque-Mexican colony was linked to its defense of its status as a preeminent community in New Spain; it was a school destined to educate the least privileged members of society, following a "traditional" educational standard. The ethnic/racial/collective element also proved vital. During the same period, the Bergara Soledad Seminary opened its doors at the heart of the Basque Enlightenment movement. Although designed in accordance with similar educational criteria, unlike the *Vizcaínas* School, it was meant only for the daughters of the region's most prosperous families.

Disputes between the Company of Mary and the Aránzazu Guild marked a period in which each organization struggled to expand its model, resulting in quarrels that were intensified back in the motherland. From an educational perspective, three models can be distinguished: that established in the *Vizcaína*s Schools and the Bergara Soledad Seminary, that developed by the Tudela, Mexico and Bergara *Enseñanzas* and that advocated by the Enlightenment movement toward the end of the century. It was the colleagues of Ignacia de Alzor who were forced to engage with the descendants and namesakes of those reformist elites who built the *Vizcaínas* School in Mexico. Finally, at the end of the nineteenth century, the members of the Aránzazu Guild adopted the pedagogical model of the *Enseñanza*, while a new generation discarded the convent-based one. The most interesting thing about all this, however, is the interactions that took place, since all parties had the opportunity of comparing themselves to each other.

This transatlantic relationship extended also to other nearby geographical and cultural locations. The project for noble ladies designed by the RSBAP was inspired by the ideas of Pablo de Olavide from Lima, as well as by the Russian institute established by Catherine the Great. This European dimension of the Basque Enlightenment movement is important to highlight, since it indicates that its members were either at the forefront of the intellectual thinking of the period, or at least in contact with it. Future studies may wish to connect that observed in the thirteen colonies and the future United States of America with the undeniably influential events that took place in Europe, as well as with what occurred in New Spain. From the perspective of women's education, understood as a process, the similarities between these contexts are evident, both in the discursive terrain in relation to the construction of femininity, and in the development of education models and the establishment of schools.

It is important to remember that, due to its charitable and non-elitist nature, the Basques settled in Mexico decided to adopt the postulates of the Company of Mary, a decision that, in reality, did not distance them from their enlightened countrymen or the new models of femininity. Proof of this lies in the close ties that developed between the Aránzazu Guild and the RSBAP.

In Mexico, the model of domestic femininity promoted by the Basque Enlightenment movement also had its advocates, most of who belonged to the reformist elite. The role played by New Spanish women during the late eighteenth century and early nineteenth century was also associated with that of "mother, support for their husband, comfort for their families and guide for their children."[6] This gender-based construct, we should remember, would permeate all privileged social groups throughout the entire seventeen-hundreds, and would spread even further as the nineteenth century wore on. In the United States of America, this image was known by the term "Republican motherhood."

In New Spain, this process came about partly thanks to the erudite press linked to economic societies, in which the Basque elite played a key role.[7] "Enlightened thinking, spread principally by the incipient modern press, enabled a greater circulation of scientific, political and economic ideas and contents, installing new platforms of sociability on which women would emerge as controversial subjects."[8]

As in the Basque Country, the education of women from the more privileged classes mainly took place at home, since there is no indication of any institutions in America similar to those established by the Basque Enlightenment movement. Although the wealthier girls of the New Spanish capital attended the *Enseñanza* school, similarly to that which occurred on the other side of the ocean, these new devices and gender stereotypes spread in an informal, non-institutionalized manner. The circulation of ideas, books, newspapers and the new Enlightened sociability was instrumental in this process. In the words of Arcos Herrera, "the press is installed as a device that has a clear pedagogical orientation within which differentiated practices for women and men are conceptualized in a multiracial and culturally heterogeneous society."[9]

The leading role played by the Mexican members of the RSBAP in the dissemination and promotion of Enlightenment culture in New Spain (such as the case of José Antonio Alzate, a Creole of Basque origin and "symbol of the Mexican Enlightenment"[10]) was not without its political consequences. The importance of the dissemination of these ideas in the Mexican independence process is evident. And the role played in the Basque community proved fundamental, turning the Basque Enlightenment movement into a transatlantic phenomenon.

Long before a Mexican political identity emerged at the beginning of the nineteenth century, a devotion-based identity already existed in the region. The veneration of figures of Basque origin, such as Saint Ignatius of Loyola and the Virgin of Aránzazu, served as integrating elements for emigrants living in New Spain. Nevertheless, these were also key promoters of a cult that would later be closely linked to the Mexican identity, namely the veneration of the Virgin of Guadalupe.

It was Archbishop Juan Antonio de Vizarrón y Eguiarreta (a fundamental supporter of the *Vizcaínas* School) who was charged with officially establishing the Virgin of Guadalupe as New Spain's patron saint in 1737.[11] This movement resulted in Belem School, which depended on the archbishopric, developing a steadfast devotion to that figure, something which, years later, would give rise to strong pro-independence sentiments—after the execution of Morelos, one of the main precursors of Independence, the schoolgirls of Belem performed a play with messages of rejection of royal authority.[12] At the opposite end of the scale was the *Vizcaínas* School, which declared itself a royalist institution.[13]

Before that (or simultaneously), Napoleon's invasion of Spain sparked a true political earthquake that shook the whole of the American continent. In response to this new situation, several members of the powerful Basque-Mexican community did everything in their power to help the motherland. This was the case, for example, with the Aguirrebengoa family, organized agents (mainly Basques[14]) located in New Spain dedicated to collecting capital, the Marquis of San Miguel de Aguayo[15] and the powerful Antonio Bassoco—he will contribute the incredible figure of 200,000 pesos.[16] Moreover, institutions such as the Aránzazu Guild, which possessed a vast amount of capital, received several demands from the Crown for "forced donations" to the cause.[17]

Linked to this, the discovery of a letter in the *Vizcaínas* archive is particularly revealing. In the letter, which was written in 1811, Gabriel de Mendizábal e Iraeta, the general in charge of the northern army fighting against Napoleon's troops, begged the Mexican ladies for aid:

"What kingdom, city, town or village has not been marked with the furor of these murders, and the heroism of its dwellers? But the border regions that are unlucky enough to inhabit the Pyrenees and their slopes and spurs, that rough land, barren in all but men who serve only to swell armies and squadrons, and who, in happier times, emigrated copiously to those lands to seek, with your favor, the fortune their own denied them, thereby forging more cordial and preferential relations and fraternity between the inhabitants in both hemispheres than with other Mediterranean dwellers on the peninsula—you will easily be able to form an idea of the misery and lack of means that afflict them [...] Oh amiable sex from foreign parts! [...] When the Republic was beset by the lack of monies and those items necessary for subsistence, the Roman ladies came together to fill the coffers of the state with their jewels and savings; and in the Third Punic War, after having worked alongside their menfolk night and day to arm and fortify the city's walls and arsenals, during the final disastrous days of Rome's rival, the ladies of Carthage severed their hair, that most precise and precious adornment, to make cords and ropes to save the relics of their dying Fleet. Would you, the ladies of Mexico and Lima, do any less? So, cooperate then, you to whom nature gave an empire that is active on men; help form, under the direction and leadership of so many prelates, clergymen and civil servants of all ranks, a fund of patriotic donations."[18]

Regardless of the response offered by the women of high American society, the disgruntlement felt by the New Spanish elite in relation to demands such as these only intensified, generating a clear feeling of discontent in the colony: "The first plan for Mexico's Independence was thought up by the owners of capital usurped by Spain."[19] It was then that the process of independence first started to take shape, giving rise to years of struggle in which the Basque elite would play an important role.

Although the *Vizcaínas* School declared itself a royalist institution, many of those linked to the RSBAP and the Aránzazu Guild came out in favor of Independence. It was the Society of Jesus, expelled from Spain in 1767, that took the lead in laying the groundwork for a Mexican identity, an "ideological movement expressed through Independence."[20] The members of the RSBAP, some of whom had been educated by the Jesuits, acted as a conveyor belt between the Society and the independence movement. However, we should not make the mistake of viewing the RSBAP as a single, homogeneous entity, since the close ties cultivated by many of its members with the Jesuits and the Company of Mary reveal an undeniable heterogeneity of both action and thought.

The list of supporters is impressive. During the independence movement led by the Mexico City Hall in 1808 (one of the first attempts at rebellion within what would prove a very long process), the Fagoaga family was divided in its loyalties, with the first Marquis of Apartado supporting the Parliament of Seville, and his heir supporting the pro-independence lobby and Viceroy Iturrigaray. This prompted the second Marquis of Apartado to make contact in the city of London with Francisco Miranda, considered one of the key precursors of Spanish-American independence. From the British capital, he also arranged to finance *El Colombiano*, a publication that supported the interests of the Americans and whose readers included the Marquis of Guardiola and the Marquis of San Miguel de Aguayo.[21]

The Navarran bishop, Juan Ruiz de Cabañas, donated 25,000 pesos to the pro-independence cause.[22] RSBAP members such as José Bernardo de Foncerrada and Francisco Xavier de Gamboa (who drafted the constitution governing the *Vizcaínas* School) were also leading figures.[23] Manuel de Aldaco, one of its founders, would later be acknowledged by Viceroy Bernardo de Gálvez as the "Father of his fatherland, Mexico."[24] Nevertheless, it was the aforementioned Fagoaga family that was one of the most active in the struggle for independence, proving instrumental in gaining the support of the British Crown for the liberation mission led by the Navarran Xavier Mina.[25]

These few examples are a telling reflection of the important role played by descendants of RSBAP members in the liberation movement. Around eighty-four individuals from this elite Enlightenment community were involved in the process, including the father of the first emperor and liberator of Mexico, José Joaquín de Iturbide.[26] In light of this situation, once independence had been obtained, "the Mexican Basques managed to preserve their former social status for various decades, retaining their place in the networks of political and financial control and conserving their one-time social authority and prestige."[27] The 1821 Act of Independence of the Mexican Empire was signed by several figures of Basque descent, including Fagoaga, Azcárate, Iturbide, Guridi y Alcocer, Velasco, Jaúregui, Icaza, Horbegoso and Echevers.[28]

Lucas Alamán, the famous nineteenth-century Mexican historian and politician, characterized the role played by this community as follows: "all the conquistadors of America, and particularly New Spain, hailed from Badajoz and Medellín in Extremadura, and all who caused the ruin of the Spanish empire established by them in the New World hailed from the Basque provinces."[29] The RSBAP, we must remember, was also born in said provinces, as was a certain Saint Ignatius of Loyola, the founder of the Society of Jesus.

But how were the educational institutions established by the Basque-Mexican elite affected by this community's support of Mexican independence? There are many indications of the stances defended by the Belem and *Vizcaína* Schools.

As a result of the changes that took place at the end of the seventeenth century in relation to the education of indigenous women, in which Spanish ethnocentrism underwent certain transformations, thereby providing this population with access to learning, at the end of the eighteenth century, *Vizcaínas* opened the doors of its Public School. Two interrelated conclusions can be drawn from this landmark event. The first is linked to the commitment made to education by the reformist elite in its "attempt to regenerate the region's social life and ensure greater economic efficiency, in which undertaking, much importance was attached to education as an instrument of progress,"[30] with the ultimate aim being that much sought-after "happiness of the Nation."

The second is related to the creolization process undergone by the Basque-Mexican community.[31] Although the *Vizcaínas* School and the Aránzazu Guild were originally created to provide support to Basque emigrants, the creolization and assimilation process undergone by many members of this community could not fail to affect the institution. Their integration into the life and dominance structures of New Spain resulted in their progressive alignment with Mexican interests, which many of the community's members then actively began to support and foster. As a result, the values defended by the Enlightenment elite focused partially on promoting the least advantaged classes, a symptom of both its creolization and its reformist nature. "The prominence acquired by education was in keeping with the search for social wellbeing and happiness; thus it began to be linked to the public domain, to society in general and to the field of the decisions made by the political authorities."[32]

We should not, however, forget those who defended the interests of the Crown, such as Antonio Bassoco, for instance, who donated 1,570,000 pesos to the fight against the uprising, a gesture that earned him the title of Count.[33] Many women of the New Spanish elite also came out on the side of the Spanish monarchy. Ana de Iraeta, a noble Creole of Basque origin, was charged with organizing the "Marian Patriots," a group of 2,500 women founded in 1810 to support the royalist cause (in light of the lack of rigorous prosopographic analyses, we can assume that this group, which was founded by the elite of the capital, had many Basque members). The principal mission of this group, which can be considered the first female society in the history of Mexico City, was to protect and take as its standard bearer the Virgin of Los Remedios, a symbol of the royalist cause embraced by pupils at the *Vizcaínas* School three years later. The group members also engaged in espionage, propaganda and funding-related activities, actions that would be acknowledged by Fernando VII himself in 1820, through the awarding of the Isabelle the Catholic Medal.[34]

Linked to monarchic power and structures despite its unconventional allegiances, Belem School served as a detention center during the struggle for independence, even housing for a time the famous María Leona Vicario.[35] For its part, the *Vizcaínas* School played host for eight months to Josefa Ortiz, who would go down in history as the person responsible for lighting the fuse of the insurrection. Not far away was the Mining School, created by the same Enlightenment thinkers linked to the RSBAP and whose students lent their support to the pro-independence cause.[36]

There are also indications of the presence of insurrectionist elements within the *Vizcaínas* School itself. The following discourse by an anonymous writer, incomplete and with no date, was found among its records:

"America is, by nature, separate from Spain, and should be so according to Justice. None of the rights to which Spain alludes for its domination are legitimate [...] after overthrowing the barbarity that reigned in centuries past, it is well known by all men, even halfwits, that to conquer a kingdom is to usurp it, to steal it. Thus, since America should not depend on Spain, those who unjustly and recklessly oppose Independence cannot faithfully call themselves the defenders of its integrity, with the title rightly belonging to them being true enemies who try to tyrannize it [...] What? Is it not a just cause to liberate our homeland from the tyrannical oppression in which it has, for the long space of three centuries, been groaning under the Spanish yoke?"[37]

Following Mexico's independence, the Aránzazu Board, the governing body of the *Vizcaínas* School, provided financial aid to the new government. Thanks to a letter from the Ministry of Taxation thanking it for its collaboration, we know that the Guild helped fund the fight against the revolt led by General Santana: "Upon learning of the financial aid sent by the Aránzazu Board to the Government of Mexico, the Emperor [the first emperor of Mexico, Agustín de Iturbide] expresses his gratitude for the four hundred pesos received."[38] Weeks later, the donation was increased to 1,000 pesos.[39]

This marked the end of an era, an era that saw the birth of different institutions established to educate women within what could be considered a transatlantic phenomenon. Despite this, however, we know next to nothing about the cultural exchanges and transfers that took place at a more individual or family level. In the future, comparative studies of private inventories and libraries may help clarify the nature of these interchanges, in both the Basque Country and America.

It should, however, be remembered that this analysis of the elite and the institutions created by them notwithstanding, it was the religious world view that was most successful in offering a valid explanation of the construction of the nature of women, understood as being inferior to that of man and descending from sinful Eve. Throughout the Enlightenment, two approaches began to interact thanks to the development of discourses inspired by Reason. From that time onward, both visions (secular and religious) existed side by side and were adapted to the needs of the moment. The question, therefore, is: within this Atlantic, transnational framework, which construction took firmer root?

As part of its response to the problems of the period, the Basque Enlightenment movement advocated the role of "good mother." With their eyes firmly set on this Enlightened utopian ideal, which was geared toward ensuring the happiness of the Nation, great ladies occupied a prominent place in the family order, helping temper customs and habits, educating their children and serving as moral benchmarks for society in general.

This utilitarian vision was based on different interconnecting elements. First, there was the idea of domestic femininity, that mother who gently and tenderly cared for and educated her offspring, exercising qualities that, according to her contemporaries, were inherent to her delicate and sensitive nature. Here, eighteenth-century discourses on sensitivity coincide with medial arguments and those referring to the role of women, both of which concur in constructing a new archetype. Engaging with their environment and supported by educational reform, we see how the mothers of this large Basque (and Mexican) Enlightenment family organized gatherings, gained prominence as musicians and expanded their knowledge. The diverse stances defended by New Spanish *novatores*, Enlightened Basques, the Society of Jesus and the Company of Mary together make up this complex scenario that spanned the Atlantic Ocean.

Observing the transformations that took place in women's education helps us understand these changes. From the second half of the eighteenth century onward, discourses such as those advocated by Pablo de Olavide and the Marquis of Montehermoso, both members of the RSBAP, projected femininity to new and hitherto unknown horizons. Moving away from religious values, secular interpretations emerged to explain the weak physical and spiritual nature of women, giving rise to a series of discourses based on sexuality. As a result, women became perfect mothers, fulfilling the role assigned to them by

Nature. From that time forwards, the women of the Basque elite, now viewed as sensitive and glorified for that exact same reason, continued to play a key role in the family order. Their access to culture, social habits and, indeed, their very significance mutated over time, although the same cannot be said of their subjugation by a society inundated with ever-changing yet always androcentric world views.

The new canon of femininity was built on unequal gender relations. At the dawn of the nineteenth century, prominent women participated in a context in which the public arena was just beginning to be built on the basis of their exclusion from it, giving rise to a male political space that justified women's absence on the basis of their lack of solidity.[40] Freedom and equality were issues that concerned only men. While the new education offered to women appreciated their targeted feelings, their honesty, modesty and virtue, the female archetype was faced with this other male culture that, through clandestine pornographic literature, "celebrated sexuality in a festive and irreverent manner, from the perspective of a male subject, showing tolerance toward all expressions of virility outside the marriage bed and representing women as stereotypical figures of transgression."[41] The culture of the period was deeply misogynous (nothing new there) and one of its leading exponents was none other than Félix María Sánchez de Samaniego, the man who proposed to establish the Vitoria House of Education for Young Ladies, author of the fables so commonly used to educate young girls, director of the Bergara Seminary and nephew of the Count of Peñaflorida.[42]

At the same time as he called for a new kind of women's education, far removed from "nunnish" instruction, the fabulist from La Rioja wrote a series of surprising narrations about sexuality, erotic relations and male/female ardor.[43] His extravagant tales, recounted for the amusement of a delighted listener, unabashedly portrayed sensual and lascivious women in contexts that, using burlesque imagery, aimed to debunk the myth of sexual coercion. This misogynous literature, which is not without passages that would today be considered incitement to rape and sexual abuse against women, was located within a framework in which men's sexual liberties and the institution of marriage and courtship seemed to be under threat. Here, gender differences are evident: for men, "decency was a strictly secular ideal of social behavior"[44]; for women, however, it was linked to religious virtues such as devotion, chastity, and piety.

By focusing on this construction of the female identity through the most novel discourses we run the risk of forgetting how they operated on or influenced the life of the vast majority of women. The educational reforms proposed by the elite groups of the time (which included new canons of femininity) were developed from, by and for the ladies of the most privileged social classes. Most women, however, never had access to the seminal treatises of the era, and their lives continued to be based on the Catholic religion and the domestic-family sphere. We should not forget that there are many other works that explore other women, other discourses and other femininities. During the eighteenth century, when change was not abrupt, categorical, or linear, various outlooks existed at the same time (something which, in itself, was a new development).

For years, these perspectives grew up around a Basque colony which strove to disseminate all manner of reformist projects, particularly economic ones.[45] On the other side of the ocean, an elite class with strong economic ties to their American compatriots started to establish the RSBAP. And in the middle, there was the Company of Mary, an organization inspired by the Society of Jesus founded by the patron saint of Guipúzcoa: Saint Ignatius, born in Loyola and namesake of the new girls' school established in Mexico.

With the passing of Xavier María de Munibe, Count of Peñaflorida, a new era began within the RSBAP; a period of change that was cut short when, in 1791, French troops once again invaded the Basque Country within the framework of the War of the Pyrenees.[46] From this moment on, the political situation grew increasingly complex, until it eventually snuffed out the great Enlightenment dream, that way of understanding life, with all its successes and failures, which proved unable to withstand the transformations that occurred in the field of transatlantic relations at the end of the eighteenth century. Subsequently, the War of Independence and the so-called Atlantic Revolutions transformed forever the web of dependency and exchange that had hitherto existed between the two shores. The Ancient Régime, the time of those men and women, began to fall into oblivion.

Reno, Nevada, 2021.

NOTES

1   Margarita Ortega López, "La educación de la mujer en la Ilustración española," *Revista de educación* extra 1 (1988): 324.
2   Urra Olazabal, *La educación*, 28-35.
3   Iker Echeberria Ayllón, *"Afectos olvidados." Mujeres de la élite vasca en el siglo XVIII* (Tesis Doctoral, UPV/EHU, 2020), 131-137.
4   Another well-known work, that of Father Feijoo. Carol Arcos Herrera, "Sujetos de controversia: aportes para una bibliografía sobre las mujeres en el siglo XVIII y la Ilustración," *Revista de Crítica Literaria Latinoamericana* 67 (2008): 112.
5   Ruiz Barrionuevo, "Libros, lectura, enseñanza," 542.
6   Mata Montes de Oca, "Mujeres," 47.
7   Alberto Saladino García, "La Real Sociedad Bascongada de los Amigos del País y las

publicaciones periódicas del siglo XVIII en Nueva España," in *IV Seminario de Historia de la Real Sociedad Bascongada de los Amigos del País. "La RSBAP y Méjico"* (Donostia-San Sebastián: RSBAP, Tomo 2, 1993), 729-736.

8 Arcos Herrera, "Sujetos de controversia," 113.
9 Arcos Herrera, "Sujetos de controversia," 115.
10 Saladino García, "La Real Sociedad," 734.
11 Muriel, "Los arzobispos vascos," 63-65.
12 *Loa en Obsequio de Nuestra Señora de Guadalupe*. Muriel, "La sociedad novohispana," 112-113.
13 Ibid., 257.
14 Gárate Ojanguren, "Remesas de capitales," 286-288.
15 AGN, Reales Cédulas Originales y Duplicados 100, Reales Cédulas Originales, Volumen 173, Expediente 87.
16 Taracena, "La migración dorada," 221.
17 García-Ayluardo, "El milagro," 455-456.
18 AHCV, Estante 6, Tabla 4, Volumen 2. Alberto Angulo Morales and Iker Echeberria Ayllón, "Herederas de la Ilustración vasca. El papel femenino en tiempos de revoluciones," in *La mujer en las revoluciones atlánticas. Roles entre la lealtad, la Ilustración y la Patria. 1795-1840*, ed. Martha Lux Martelo and Alejandro Cardozo Uzcátegui, Alejandro (Bogotá: Universidad Sergio Arboleda, in press).
19 Guadalupe Jiménez Codinach, "Algunos miembros de la Real Sociedad Bascongada y sus descendientes, amigos de la Independencia de la Nueva España," in *IV Seminario de Historia de la Real Sociedad Bascongada de los Amigos del País. "La RSBAP y Méjico"* (Donostia-San Sebastián: RSBAP, Tomo 2, 1993), 845.
20 Torales Pacheco, *Ilustrados*, 188.
21 Méndez Reyes, "Los Fagoaga," 297-302.
22 Muriel, "Los arzobispos vascos," 69-71.
23 Jiménez Codinach, "Algunos miembros," 846 and 849.
24 Ibid., 849.
25 Ibid., 851.
26 Ibid., 861-869.
27 Ludlow Wiechers, "Los vascos-mexicanos," 910.
28 Guadalupe Pérez San Vicente, *Análisis Paleográfico sobre el Acta de Independencia* (México: UNAM, 1961), 3-4.
29 Lucas Alamán, *Historia de Méjico* (México: Editorial Jus, Volume 1, 1968), 229.
30 Zoraida Vázquez, "La educación," 12.
31 Luque Alcaide, "Asociacionismo vasco," 78.
32 Arcos Herrera, "Sujetos de controversia," 114.
33 Taracena, "La migración dorada," 221.
34 Ivana Frasquet, "Actrices en la independencia de México: buscando su lugar en la Historia," in *Jamás ha llovido reyes del cielo. De independencias, revoluciones y liberalismos en Iberoamérica*, ed. Ivana Frasquet (Quito: Corporación Editorial Nacional, 2013), 218; Muriel, "La sociedad novohispana," 257; Celia Palacio Montiel, "La participación femenina en la Independencia de México," in *Historia de las mujeres en México* (México: Instituto Nacional de Estudios Históricos de las Revoluciones de México, 2015), 87.

35 Ana Belén García López, "La participación de las mujeres en la independencia hispanoamericana a través de los medios de comunicación," *Historia y Comunicación Social* 16 (2011): 39; Muriel, "La sociedad novohispana," 109-110.
36 Ibid., 257.
37 AHCV, Estante 6, Tabla 4, Volumen 2.
38 Mexico City, 12/24/1822. Letter from the Minister of Finance Medina to José María de Echave. AHCV, Estante 15, Tabla 2, Volumen 2.
39 Mexico City, 01/14/1823. Letter from the Minister of Finance Medina to José María de Echave. AHCV, Estante 15, Tabla 2, Volumen 2.
40 Nerea Aresti Esteban, "Los argumentos de la exclusión. Mujeres y liberalismo en la España contemporánea," *Historia Constitucional* 13 (2012): 407-414.
41 Mónica Bolufer Peruga, "La realidad y el deseo: formas de subjetividad femenina en la época moderna," in *Mujer y deseo: representaciones prácticas de vida*, ed. María José de la Pascua, María del Rosario García-Doncel and Gloria Espigado (Cádiz: Universidad de Cádiz, 2004), 370.
42 Ibid., 370. Samaniego's stories resemble Moratín's. Gloria Franco Rubio, "Nicolás Fernández de Moratín y El arte de las putas," in *Feminismo y misoginia en la literatura española. Fuentes literarias para la Historia de las Mujeres*, ed. Cristina Segura Graíño (Madrid: Narcea, 2001), 97-122.
43 Félix María de Samaniego [editing by Emilio Palacios Fernández], *El jardín de Venus y otros jardines de verde hierba* (Madrid: Ediciones Siro, 1976).
44 Benedetta Craveri, "La contribución de las mujeres a una nueva forma de civilidad (ss. XVII-XVIII)," in *Educar los sentimientos y las costumbres. Una mirada desde la historia*, ed. Mónica Bolufer, Carolina Blutrach and Juan Gomis (Zaragoza: Institución Fernando el Católico, CSIC, 2014), 139.
45 Palacios Fernández, "Proyección," 54-57.
46 Álvaro Aragón Ruano, "La Guerra de la Convención, la separación de Guipúzcoa y los comerciantes vasco-franceses y bearneses," *Pedralbes. Revista d'historia moderna* 31 (2011): 167-232; Cirilo Chico Comerón, "La Guerra de la Convención en Guipúzcoa (1793-1795): daños causados por las tropas francesas," *Espacio, Tiempo y Forma, Serie IV, Historia Moderna* 24 (2011): 175-187.

APPENDIX

Table 1: National Brotherhoods Established in Madrid

Space	Zone	Congregations	Dates
Castile	Cantabric zone	Navarros, vascos, montañeses, gallegos, riojanos and asturianos	1683-1743
Aragon	Crown of Aragon	Aragonese, Catalans and Valencians	1728-1745
America	Peru and México	Santo Toribio and Nuestra Señora de Guadalupe	1727-1743
Castile	Old Castile	Castilians and Leonese, La Rioja, Burgos, Seguntinos and Madrilenians	1727-1752
Castile	New Castile	Coquenses, Manchego, Toledo and Andalusians	1748-1793

Source: Angulo Morales, "Los frutos," 130.

Table 2: Donors to the Colegio de las Vizcaínas, 1731-1735

Donor	Pesos	Donor	Pesos
Juan Antonio de Vizarrón y Eguiarreta, arzobispo México	6,000	Ignacio Antonio Bustamante	25
Doctor Martín de Elizacoechea	2,400	Francisco de Zupide y Acuña	25

Basque Women's Education in the 18th Century

Donor	Pesos	Donor	Pesos
José de Aguirre y Elizondo y María del Rey	1,500	José de la Fuente	300
Josefa de Arozqueta y Francisco de Fagoaga	2,500	María de Estrada	200
Francisco de Echeveste	2,000	Lorenzo de Zubia	25
Migue de Amassorrain	1,500	Juan Francisco de Vertiz	50
José de Garate	1,000	Reparaz	50
Manuel de Iriarte	1,000	José de Elizalde	100
Sebastián de Verin y Seyras	25	José Antonio de Zavala	200
Isidro Navarro	200	Matías de Aldaz	100
Antonio Sarasola	100	Juan Ángel de Urra	100
Agustín de Palma y Mesa	400	Pedro de GAnuza	100
Juan Agustín de Portu	300	Francisco de Achiga	50
Ignacio de Michelena	500	Domingo de Gomendio	500
Martín de Valencia y Zavalza	200	José de Lopeola	100
Gorostiaga	500	José de Garaicoechea	100
Eliza	400	Juan Antonio Sánchez Lenero	50
José Antonio de Leiza	300	Antonio de Villar y Lanzagorta	50
Manuel de Agesta	1,000	Martín de Mutio	100
Fernando de Ugarte	400	Manuel de Ezchari	50
Teresa de Zaldívar	500	Juan de Ymas	50
Brigadier Francisco de Zaldívar	500	Juan José de Echeverria	50
Bernardino de Vizarrón	300	Juan Roldán	50
Francisco Felipe de Egiara	500	Lorenzo de Inchaurregui y Manuel de Arvide	150
Valdiviezo	500	Manuel de Aldaco	300
Juan Domingo de Oteiza	50	Conde de Miravalle	50
Cayetano de Medina y Saravia	200	Pedro de Echenique	50
Aziburu	200	Bernardo Yun y Barvia	25
Echevarria	100	Domingo de Vertiz	200
Ugarte	200	Pablo de Meoqui	50
Camino y Vergara	100	Nicolasa María de San José	1,5 R
Salgado	50	Francisco Antonio de Yocano	25

Donor	Pesos	Donor	Pesos
Juan José de Arpide	1,000	Juan de Arizavalo	50
Juan Xavier Gastón de Iriarte, Martín Baquedano, Andrés Velarde y Sola y Alonso Velázquez Gastelu	100	José de Lansagorta	300
Aristoarena	300	José de Echeandia	500
Mercero Iriarte	200	Juan de Ibarrola	200
Fernando de Gradi	50	Pedro de Inchaurreta	50
Antonio de Llantada Ybarra	300	Manuel de Orendayn	50
Alejandro Vitorica	200	Francisco de Garro	50
Iturbide	600	Marco Antonio de Vaquedano	50
Alarburu	100	Juan de Iturrondo	100
Medina	100	Pedro de Echeverria y Delgado	100
Juan Miguel de Echeverria	300	Miguel de Aldave	50
Ana María de Echeverria	100	Agustín de Iñurrigarro	400
Guraia	500	Francisco de Murguiondo	100
Villar	200	Joaquín González	50
José de Foroz	100	Juan de Arosqueta	100
Martín de Echarte	200	Domingo de Osoategui	100
Pedro de Urzúa	500	Antonio de Zavala	25
Juan Pastor de Olimares	100	Juan de Torres	200
Doctor Ubilla	100	Pedro Bringas	50
Juan Domingo Antón	50	Matías Cano	25
Juan Bautista de Pradas	100	Justo Bolado y Muñoz	200
Francisco de Zavalza	25	Juana de Silva y Portillo	Pendientes
Manuel de Gorenechea	100	Francisco de Urtussautegui	300
Antonio de Azterrica	25	Domingo de Urtussautegui	150
Francisco de Azcue	50	Manuel de Alcedo	50
Francisco Santos Rodrigo	25	Basilio de Arrillaga y Ezeiza	25
Miguel de Arriquibar	25	Pedro Bueno de Bassori	500
Felipe de Recarte	50	Antonio de Echeandia	200
Juan Antonio de Veldarrain	25	Santiago de Zerrillo	12
Bentura de Aldecoa	50	Juan Bentura de Salazar	12
Roque de Andonaegui	100	José Francisco de Aguirre	500

Donor	Pesos	Donor	Pesos
Juan Antonio de Beica	50	Manuel de Sein	50
Nicolás de Marreategui	50	Pedro de Negrete Sierra	200
Manuel de la Vega	50	Esteban de Larreburu	150
Pedro de Sagasta	50	Gonzalo de Leagui	25
Felipe José de Narvarte	50	Diego de Orozco	25
Juan Bautista de Zuaznavar	25	José Rodríguez Mauriño	25
Nicolás de Zengotita Ybarra	100	José de la Cámara Enssiso	25
Juan de Ugarte	50	Miguel de Gambarte	50
Francisco de Gomiciaga	50	Francisco Antonio del Campo	25
Doctor Martín de Urtussaustegui	100	Juan Martín de Arizcun	25
Tomás de Lercundi	50	José de Sassorena	25
Juan de Urizar y Silva	25	Enrique de Atocha	25
Juan Antonio de Olavarria	100	Margarita Amassorrain	25
Bartolomé de Arizaga	50	Francisco de Villar Gutierrez	20
Francisco Ortiz de Manzaneda	25	Cristóbal de Llanos	15
Juan González y María Marcela de la Peña	25	Francisco de Macuzo	10
Manuel de la Puente	100	Martín de Gamboa	5
Pablo de Arizavalo	25	José de la Puente	10
José de Urbina	100	Domingo del Campo	200
Reimundo de Sequera	25	José de Landa	10
Luis de Luindo	150	Tomás de Guridi	12
José Aranguren y Manuel Sainz	25	Ignacio Valcárcel	25
José Antonio Udran y Vitoria	25	Diego de Monterde	25
José de Castañeda y Mendiburu	100	José de la Peña	20
Domingo de Alegría	25	Juan Martín de Arechaga	50
Doctor Manuel Antonio Luiando	50	José de Gorraez	100
José de Meave	15	Miguel de Abaytua	50
Francisco Mirabelide y Casadevante	12	Sebastián de Aguirre y Gomendio	25
TOTAL			41.496

Source: own elaboration from AHCV, Estante 5, Tabla V, Volumen 7.

Table 3: Testamentary donations of General Francisco de Echeveste

Donation	Pesos
Alms for people in need to deliver to the archbishop	4,000
To the Company of Mary, the Enseñanza	10,000
Poor Capuchinas	6,000
Congregation of Oratorio de San Felipe Neri	6,000
Convent of Santo Domingo	2,000
Tabernacle of the convent of Santo Domingo	1,000
Hospital of the Third Order of San Francisco	4,000
Real Colegio de Cristo	500
Sacristies of nine convents	4,500
Convent of San Fernando	1,500
Archconfraternity of Santo Sacramento de la Santa Catedral	2,000
Convent of Bethlemitas	10,000
Convent of San Agustín	6,000
Carmelitas de San Joaquín School	5,000
Convent of Carmelitas de San Sebastián	2,000
Convent of Religiosos de la Merced de las Huertas	2,000
Oil lamp of the convent of the Merced de las Huertas	1,000
Convent of Santa Teresa la Nueva	4,000
Hospital of San Jacinto	2,000
Hospice of Santo Tomás de Villanueva	2,000
Colegiata of Nuestra Señora de Guadalupe	5,000
La salve, every Saturday, to Nuestra Señora de Aránzazu (convent of San Francisco)	5,000
School and hospital San Pedro	2,000
Convent of Santa Brígida	2,000
Sor Gertrudis Margarita Echeveste, novice in the convent of Santa Clara	2,300
María Bernarda Jiménez de Velasco, novice in the Enseñanza	500
Three mass chaplaincies (3,000 pesos each)	9,000
Three mass chaplaincies (3,000 pesos each)	9,000
Six mass chaplaincies (3,000 pesos each)	18,000
Three mass chaplaincies (3,000 pesos each)	9,000
Complete the pious work of Miguel de Amasorrain in the convent of San Francisco	330

Attorney General of the Holy Rosary Province of the Philippine Islands	16,000
Royal House of Holy Mercy of Manila	50,000
Chapel of the Third Order of San Francisco	5,000
Hospital church of San Lázaro	2,000
Hospital of San Juan de Dios	10,000
Hospital of San Lázaro	6,000
Convent of San Francisco	1,000
Third Order of San Francisco	2,000
For "legatees he names"	4,269
Three chapels in Usúrbil (3,000 each)	9,000
Redeem a lien in Usurbil	5,000
Mass chapel	4,000
Mass chapel	4,000
Masses	1,217
Available to his friends and executors	80,000
Give freedom to his slaves María Baltasara, Ignacia Teresa and María Teresa	–
Manufacture and send silver pieces to the parish church of Usúrbil	–
Repair of the vaults and tower of the parish church of Usúrbil	–
Erecting a chapel in the community of Aguinaga	–
TOTAL	**334,116**

Source: own elaboration from AGN, Bienes Nacionales, Volumen 49, Expediente 116.

TABLE 4: SAMPLE OF LOANS GRANTED BY THE COLEGIO DE LAS VIZCAÍNAS

Comerciante	Pesos
Juan Castañiza	3,000
Juan Bautista de Aldasoro	15,000
Severino de Arechavala	6,000
Adrián de Larramendia	14,000
Matías de Miramontes	60,000
Francisco de Corres	45,000
TOTAL	**143,000**

Source: AGNCM, Escribano Agustín Francisco Guerrero y Tagle, Notaría 268, Volumen 1723 and Volumen 1724.

Appendix 5: Letter from the Count of Peñaflorida to Pedro Jacinto de Álava[4]

"Querido Pedro Jacinto: como acá me sobra tiempo para echar mis concertados sueños, acabo de hacer uno a resueltas de las continuas conversaciones que he tenido con Salcedo [...] y aunque me hago cargo del poco aprecio que merecen los sueños, quiero contarte el mío antes que se me borren las especies empezando por su origen.

Este ha sido el cuasi continuo coloque que hemos tenido sobre las grandes dificultades que un Caballero particular encuentra para dar salida a sus hijas [...] no pudiendo pensarse en Casarlas sin buenas dotes [...] De aquí vinimos a parar la consideración en el dolor de los Padres sensibles al ver avanzar en años a sus hijas sin esperanza de mejorar de suerte, sino antes bien condenadas a esclavizarse a cuñadas o Madrastras, y perpetuarse con el triste y despreciable carácter de Damas viejas o Feas [...] la desgracia mayor que puede ocurrir a una Mujer es el haber nacido en el gremio de la Nobleza.

Esta dolorosa pero evidente consecuencia nos ha llevado a serias reflexiones sobre el modo de remediar tan grave daño político; pero por más que hemos apurado la materia solo se nos han presentado tres medios que se ofrecen a cualquiera a primera vista: el 1º mover los ánimos piadosos y ricos a fundaciones de dotes para doncellas nobles: el 2º vencer la repugnancia que se tiene en beneficiar (digámoslo así) la Nobleza distinguida, comunicándola por casamientos y con ahorro de dotes a familias de inferior calidad: y el 3º establecer comunidades de Señoras que no sean de Monjas como las que se ven particularmente en los Países bajos y la Alemania. El primero de estos medios es muy largo de verificarse aun cuando se pensase en él por las inmensas capitalidades que se necesitarían para fundaciones pías de dotes tan cuantiosas como se exigen hoy de las Señoritas: el 2º ocasionaría grandísimos sentimientos en la Parentela y acaso perjuicios reales en el Estado: y así solo el tercero es el en que puede pensarse para que las que no aspiran a ser Monjas y no tienen proporción para Casadas, tengan a lo menos un asilo honroso que les proporcione en el Cuerpo del Estado una Clase distinguida y de estimación. Pero ¿de qué sirve el pensar en esto? ¿En dónde se hallarán medios para fundar en el País un Establecimiento de estos? Aquí entra mi Sueño.

La Monja fundadora de Vergara, me han asegurado ha obtenido Bula de su Santidad [...] pero el Ministerio está y estará seguramente firme en no consentir semejante fundación [...] si una persona Religiosa o Económica de carácter y de la confianza de la Monja la convenciese plenamente de la imposibilidad de la fundación de Vergara [...] si pues hubiese persona capaz de pintar con vivos colores todo esto, no me parece imposible el que se calentase en esta idea y se resolviese a ofrecer para el nuevo Instituto sus caudales [...].

Logrado esto, que no me parece imposible, lo sería menos el Establecimiento indicado, no bajo el título de Canónigas Económicas como las Comunidades de Señoras de Países Extranjeros, sino con el de Institutoras y Ayudantas de la Superiora, a quien profesarían subordinación por juramento mientras no saliesen del Colegio para tomar Estado u otro partido que las acomodase. La superiora sólo por esta vez y por la recomendación de fundadora podría ser Religiosa, y las Ayudantas de Número o indotadas podrían ser seis [...].

Estas Señoras no tendrían obligación de dedicarse a Ministras sino en interinatos, pero no serían incompatibles sus ministerios con los de Maestras, siempre que se hallase aptitud en ellas [...]. El objeto principal de ellas sería el de servir de Inspectoras o Institutora en virtud y modales, y de componer bajo la Presidencia de la superiora una Junta privada de nuestra Sociedad.

Este mi sueño: y como estoy acostumbrado a ver verificados otros menos verosímiles que han ocurrido entre nosotros, no he querido quedarme con él en el Cuerpo; mas que no produzca otro efecto que el de divertirte con su lectura."

TABLE 6: MOST RELEVANT MARRIAGES OF THE URBINA HOUSE (EIGHTEENTH-NINETEENTH CENTURY)

Marriages	Dowries Brought to Marriage	Arras
Brígida Ortiz de Zárate González de Junguitu 1713	44,000 reales de vellón on account of legitimate maternal.	1000 reales
Bartolomé Ortiz de Urbina Ruiz de Zurbano	60,000 reales de vellón. Main heir.	
Gregoria de Urbina Zárate 1732	6,000 escudos of silver (91,500 reales).	Eighth part of the dowry
Antonio Manuel de Hinojedo Desojo	Universal heir to family property.	
Engracia de Urbina Zárate 1738	7,000 escudos of silver (105,000 reales)	2,000 ducados (22,000 reales)
José Joaquín Barroeta y Aldamar	Family elders. Undetermined value.	
Joaquina Gaytán de Ayala Larzanguren 1749	8,000 ducados (88,000 reales) + Legitimate paternal and maternal that was to inherit.	4,000 reales.
Juan Manuel de Urbina Zárate	40,000 reales	
Ramón María de Urbina Gaytán de Ayala 1787	Legitimate paternal and future maternal. Main heir.	—
María Mercedes Ferraz y Pereda	1,000,000 reales.	
Ramón María de Urbina Gaytán de Ayala 1796	Legitimate paternal and future maternal. Main heir.	—
Manuela de Salazar Sánchez de Samaniego	20,000 ducados (220,000 reales). Later, 501,000 reales in total are calculated.	
Teotiste María de Urbina Salazar 1815	Universal heiress of the family assets + 300,000 reais of dowry in case a future male is born.	4,000 ducados
Iñigo José Ortés de Velasco Esquíbel	Improved main heir in "tercio y quinto".	

Source: own elaboration from AMA.

Table 7: Some works belonging to the Urbina family library

Brígida Ortiz de Zárate González de Junguitu Finales XVII-1747.	*Mística Ciudad de Dios, Vida de Santa Teresa de Jesús, Confesiones de San Agustín, La Familia Regulada, Ejercicios del padre Rodríguez, Luz de verdades Católicas,* *Catecismo Romano, Teatro Crítico Universal.*
Joaquina Gaytán 1731-1806.	*Historia de España por Mariana, Vida de San Francisco de Sales, Agricultura del prior Croiset año a año en francés falto en cuatro tomos, Mística Ciudad de Dios, Reglamento de Monte Pío, Vida del padre Francisco Gerónimo, Arte de repostería y cocina, Décadas de la Guerra Santa, Mes Eucaristeo, Pensamientos Cristianos, Memorias de intriga en la Corte, Curiosidades con Naturaleza, El Jardinero Solícito, Meditaciones de Bosuet, Vida devota de San Francisco de Sales, dos tomos de estudios para Damas, Historia Universal en francés, Historia de Cosas memorables en España, Fuente Sucesión pontificia falto en cuatro tomos, Historia de Carlos V, Manual de Cuaresma, Memorias de la Condesa en Corte, Tratado de la Penitencia en francés.*
Manuela de Salazar Sánchez de Samaniego 1779-1844.	*Sobre educación de los niños, Método para criar niños, La Familia Regulada, El Estudiante Virtuoso, Geografía de los niños, El ayo de la juventud christiana de ambos sexos o Biblioteca completa de Educación, El espíritu del bello sexo, La mujer feliz, Instrucción de la mujer cristiana, Almacén de las señoritas cristianas, Los estudios convenientes a las señoritas o Nestorianismo para las damas, La mujer feliz dependiente del mundo y de la fortuna, Discurso sobre la educación física y moral de las mujeres, Biblioteca completa de educación o instrucciones para las señoras jóvenes, Tratado de educación de las hijas, Manual de las señoritas o arte para aprender cuantas habilidades constituyen el verdadero mérito de las mujeres, Consejos a las niñas, Eufemia o la mujer verdaderamente instruida.*
Teotiste María de Urbina Salazar 1797-1825. *Most of the works belonging to the family library were acquired between 1760 and 1830. Due to the premature death of Teotiste, we deduce that a good part of the copies inventoried at his death were obtained by his ancestors.	*Principios geográficos, El espíritu del bello sexo, El ayo de juventud cristiana, Sobre educación de los niños, Eufemia, cartas de Emeranza, Fabulas de Samaniego, Reflexiones sobre la naturaleza, La Perfecta casada, Historia de Pío sexto, Método para criar niños, Apología de la lengua vascongada, La Familia Regulada, El estudiante virtuoso, La mujer feliz, Instrucciones de la mujer cristiana, Almacén (el nacer) de los niños, Almacén de las señoritas adolescentes, Biblioteca completa de educación, Geografía de los niños, Conversaciones familiares, Los estudios convenientes a las señoritas, Nuevos cuentos morales de Madama Beanuret, Consentimiento paterno en los matrimonios, Buchan medicina doméstica, Nestorianismo Para las damas, Demostración del teatro crítico universal por Feijoo, Instrucción al primero y segundo tomo del Teatro Crítico, Justa repulsa de acusaciones por Feijoo, Cartas Eruditas en que se continúa el designio del Teatro Crítico.*

Source: Own elaboration from Luis Berasategui Garaizábal, Biblioteca Alameda. La biblioteca de una familia ilustrada en Vitoria (Vitoria: Manuscrito, 2004).

Table 8: Various works belonging to the Gortázar family

Fechas	Obras
1750-1850	*Desengaños Místicos de Antonio Arbiol; La Familia Regulada; Obras de Feijoo.*
1756	*Obras del padre Feijoo; Impugnación al Teatro Crítico de Feijoo por Salvador José Mañier.*
1775-1850	*Telémaco de Fénelon; Historia del famoso predicador Fray Gerundio de Campazas, alias el Zotes del padre Isla; Teatro Crítico de Feijoo; Ilustración apologética de Sarmiento; Cartas eruditas de Feijoo; Recherches sur les habillemens des femmes et des enfans.*
1790-1810	*El amigo de la juventud; Cartas de Madame Sévigné; Educación de la juventud; Consentimiento paterno; Educación popular; Discurso sobre la honra y deshonra; obras completas de Feijoo; Consideraciones sobre las costumbres del siglo; Vida de Madame Chantal.*
1808-1809	*Sobre la educación física de las mujeres*

Source: AHFB, Fondo Gortázar, 2492/033, 2492/030, 2492/032, 2441/011 and 2443/006.

Table 9: Distribution of books between the Gortázar sisters, 1821

Juliana	El don Quijote, Catecismo de Poujet, Garcés Lengua Castellana, Arte de pintura, Constante amarillo, Vida de San Francisco de Sales, Diálogo del diseño, Tablas poéticas, Cartas teológicas, Los eruditos a la violeta, Historia sacramental, literatura, Journalist, Lambert, Noches de invierno, Milagro de nuestra Señora de Begoña, Modelo de letras en francés, Aforismos de Niremberg, Erasto, Voces del pastor, Diccionario filosófico, Catecismo de Flauri, Reformación cristiana, Curia filípica, Consideraciones sobre los novísimos.
María Dolores	La Biblia, Viaje a Constantinopla, Fueros de Vizcaya, Discurso sobre la educación de las mujeres, Croixet discurso espiritual, Aventuras de Telémaco, Mondejar Historia de España, Institución militar cristiana, Diccionario de la fábula, Curiosidades de la naturaleza, Gritos del purgatorio, Conversación de la salud de los pueblos, Gramática castellana, Descripción del nuevo planetario.
Josefa Gabriela	Diccionario histórico, Vida de San Agustín, Viaje de Magallanes, Manifiesto de Vizcaya, Fueros de Vizcaya, Leyes de Navarra, Establecimientos, Cervantes, Recreaciones políticas, Fábulas de Samaniego, Millot Historia Universal, Geografía manual, Ordenanzas militares, Ercilla, Recreaciones físicas, Arte de repostería, Catecismo de Fleuri en pergamino, Villareal de Molinos, Economía política.
Nicolasa Irene	Novelas de Cervantes, Viaje al Parnaso, Veladas de la quinta, Representación al rey, Apología de la lengua vascongada, Diferencia entre lo temporal y eterno, Catalogía de Ytariet, Diccionario geográfico histórico de España, Diccionario de Arquitectura, Mesa camino y posada, El evangelio en triunfo, Diccionarios de Gatel, Diccionario geográfico, Diccionario de bellas artes, Retiro espiritual, Catón español, Servicios de Bilbao, Blanchiman, Tratado de la Peste, Juan de la Encina, Historia de pintores, Devoción arreglada

Source: AHFB, Fondo Gortázar, 2443/017.

Notes

1. In 1743, he bought a 25-year-old black slave named María Josefa from a certain Agustín Juárez de Miranda. This is how she describes her sales contract: "he bought soul in mouth and bones in sack." When this Agustín de Juárez bought her from a factor of the Royal Seat of Great Britain, she was 14 years old. AGNCM, Escribano Nicolás Ubaldo Benítez Trigueros, Notaría 76, Volumen 520. María Elisa Velázquez Gutiérrez, Mujeres de origen africano en la capital novohispana, siglos XVII y XVIII (*México D.F.: Instituto Nacional de Antropología e Historia, UNAM, 2006*).
2. AGN, Bienes Nacionales, Volumen 49, Expediente 116; Pablo de Gorosabel, Diccionario histórico-geográfico-descriptivo de los *pueblos, valles, partidos, alcaldías y uniones de Guipúzcoa (Tolosa: Imprenta de Pedro Gurruchaga, 1862)*, 5.
3. Ana Rita Valero de García Lascuráin, Baltazar Brito Gaudarrama and Juan Carlos Franco Montes de Oca, Don Fr*ancisco, 14.*
4. Letter from Xabier María de Munibe to Pedro Jacinto de Álava, Logroño, 06/25/1784. APV, Fondo Álava, legajo 3.

BIBLIOGRAPHY

Aguilar Piñal, Francisco. Bibliografía de la Real Sociedad Vascongada de los Amigos del País en el siglo XVIII. San Sebastián: CSIC, 1971.
Aguinagalde, Borja de. "La fundación de la Real Sociedad Bascongada de los Amigos del País ¿un asunto de familia?." In *II Seminario de Historia de la Real Sociedad Bascongada de Amigos del País*, 395-444. Donostia-San Sebastián: RSBAP, 1988.
———. Guía para la reconstrucción de familias en Guipúzcoa (XV-XIX). Donostia: Gipuzkoako Foru Aldundia, 1994.
Alamán, Lucas. *Historia de Méjico*. México: Editorial Jus, Volume 1, 1968.
Alcorta Ortiz de Zárate, Elena. La burguesía mercantil en el Bilbao del siglo XVIII. Los Gómez de la Torre y Mazarredo. San Sebastián: Txertoa, 2003.
———."La importancia del comercio en el siglo XVIII y su influencia en la RSBAP." In *Ilustración, ilustraciones*, edited by Jesús Astigarraga Goenaga, María Victoria López-Cordón Cortezo and José María Urquía Echave, 953-966. Madrid: Sociedad Estatal de Conmemoraciones Culturales, Volume 2, 2009.
Alonso Seoane, María José. "El último sueño de Pablo de Olavide." *Cuadernos Dieciochistas* 4 (2003): 47-65.
Altonaga, Bakarne. "Mujeres viriles en el siglo XVIII. La construcción de la feminidad por el discurso foralista de Manuel de Larramendi." *Historia Contemporánea* 52 (2016): 9-42.
Álvarez Gila, Óscar and Alberto Angulo Morales. *Las migraciones vascas en perspectiva histórica (siglos XVI-XX)*. Bilbao: UPV/EHU, 2002.
Amezaga Iribarren, Arantzazu. "La Real Compañía Guipuzcoana de Caracas. Crónica sentimental con una visión historiográfica. Los años áuricos y las rebeliones (1728-1751)." *Sancho el Sabio. Revista de cultura e investigación vasca* 23 (2005): 167-208.
Amezaga, Vicente de. *Hombres de la Compañía Guipuzcoana*. Bilbao: Editorial La Gran Enciclopedia Vasca, Volume II, 1979.
Amorós Puente, Celia. "Simone de Beauvoir: entre la vindicación y la crítica al Androcentrismo." *Investigaciones Feministas* 0 (2009): 9-27.
Ampudia de Haro, Fernando. "Cortesía y prudencia: una gestión civilizada del comportamiento y de las emociones." In *Accidentes del alma. Las emociones en la Edad Moderna*, edited by María Tausiet and James S. Amelang, 123-143. Madrid: Abada Editores, 2009.
Andrés Ucendo, José Ignacio. "El trabajo femenino en el Bilbao de 1824." In *Historia de la mujer e historia del matrimonio*, edited by María Victoria López-Cordón and Montserrat Carbonell Esteller, 317-326. Murcia: Universidad de Murcia, 1997.
Angulo Morales, Alberto e Iker Echeberria Ayllón. "Herederas de la Ilustración vasca. El papel

femenino en tiempos de revoluciones." In *La mujer en las revoluciones atlánticas. Roles entre la lealtad, la Ilustración y la Patria. 1795-1840*, edited by Martha Lux Martelo and Alejandro Cardozo Uzcátegui, Alejandro. Bogotá: Universidad Sergio Arboleda, en prensa.

Angulo Morales, Alberto and Álvaro Aragón Ruano (Ed.). Recuperando el Norte. Empresas, capitales y proyectos atlánticos en la economía imperial hispánica. Bilbao: UPV/EHU, 2016.

Angulo Morales, Alberto. Del éxito en los negocios al fracaso del Consulado. La formación de la burguesía mercantil de Vitoria (1670-1840). Bilbao: UPV/EHU, 2000.

_____. De Cameros a Bilbao. Negocios, familia y nobleza en tiempos de crisis (1770-1834). Bilbao: UPV/EHU, 2007.

_____. "Otro "imposible vencido": hombres, provincias y reinos en la Corte en tiempos de Carlos II." In *Volver a la «hora navarra». La contribución navarra a la construcción de la monarquía española en el siglo XVIII*, edited by Rafael Torres Sánchez, 33-72. Pamplona: Universidad de Navarra, 2010.

_____. "Embajadores, agentes, congregaciones y conferencias: la proyección exterior de las provincias vascas (siglos XV-XIX)." In *Delegaciones de Euskadi (1936-1975). Antecedentes históricos de los siglos XVI al XIX, origen y desarrollo*, 23-98. Vitoria-Gasteiz: Gobierno Vasco-Eusko Jaurlaritza, 2010.

_____. "Mercados y financieros vascos. El circuito de la plata y su control en el Seiscientos." In *Tesoreros, "arrendadores" y financieros en los reinos hispánicos. La Corona de Castilla y el Reino de Navarra (siglos XIV-XVII)*, edited by Ernesto García Fernández, 241-256. Madrid: Ministerio de Economía y Hacienda, Instituto de Estudios Fiscales, 2012.

_____. "Las geografías epistolares de las élites vascongadas y la formación de comunidades ilustradas en el siglo XVIII: la Real Congregación de San Ignacio y la Real Sociedad Bascongada de los Amigos del País." In *"Las cartas las inventó el afecto." Ensayos sobre epistolografía en el Siglo de las Luces*, edited by Rafael Padrón Fernández, 47-80. Santa Cruz de Tenerife: Ediciones Idea, 2013.

_____. "De la congregación de Cantabria o San Ignacio al proyecto de la Bascongada. El grupo de presión vasco en la Villa y Corte de Madrid (1713-1775)." In *Devoción, paisanaje e identidad. Las cofradías y congregaciones de naturales en España y en América (siglos XVI-XIX)*, edited by Óscar Álvarez Gila, Alberto Angulo Morales, Alberto and Jon Ander Ramos Martínez, 199-226. Bilbao: UPV/EHU, 2014.

_____. "Los frutos de la movilidad. La emigración norteña peninsular en Madrid y el Imperio (siglos XVII y XVIII)." *Obradoiro de Historia Moderna* 24 (2015): 113-139.

_____. "Los hidalgos norteños en el centro de un Imperio: Madrid (1638-1850). Negocios, política e identidad." In *Recuperando el Norte: empresas, capitales y proyectos atlánticos en la economía imperial hispánica*, edited by Alberto Angulo Morales and Álvaro Aragón Ruano, 261-296. Bilbao: UPV/EHU, Bilbao, 2016.

_____. "Migration, Mobility and Voyages. A Case Study on the Use of Private Sources for the Understanding of Basque Migration in the Eighteenth Century." In *From the Records of my Deepest Memory. Personal Sources and the Study of European Migration, eighteenth-20th centuries*, edited by Óscar Álvarez Gila and Alberto Angulo Morales, 13-40. Bilbao: UPV/EHU, 2016.

_____. "Des hommes, des idées, et des ressources: le projet de la *Bascongada* et la Congrégation royale des trois provinces de Cantabrie à Madrid (1713-1775)." In *Savoir et civisme. Les sociétés savantes et l'action patriotique en Europe au XVIIIe siècle*, edited by Michèle Cogriez Labarthe, Juan Manuel Ibeas Altamira et Alain Schorderet, 379-388. Genève: Slatkine Érudition, 2017.

_____. "Información, negociación y defensa. Las fronteras en las provincias exentas (XVI-XVII)." In *Dinámica de las fronteras en periodos de conflicto. El Imperio español (1640-1815)*, edited by Miguel Ángel Melón Jiménez, Miguel Rodríguez Cancho e Isabel Testón Núñez, 153-171. Cáceres: Universidad de Extremadura, 2019.

_____. "El *institutional entangled global network* de navarros y vascongados en la defensa atlántica por la plata peruana del Seiscientos (Madrid, Potosí y Puno)." *Protohistoria* 35 (2021): 361-378.

_____. "De la familia provincial a la atlántica: hijos de las Provincias y Señorío. Reputación y éxito en la movilidad norteña (XVI-XIX)." In *Familias, trayectorias, desigualdades. Estudios de historia social en España y en Europa ss. XVI-XIX*, edited by Francisco García González, 179-200. Madrid: Sílex, 2021.

_____. "El *institutional entangled global network* de navarros y vascongados en la defensa atlántica por la plata peruana del Seiscientos (Madrid, Potosí y Puno)." *Protohistoria* 35 (2021): 361-378.

Aparicio, Celia María. "Los bienes de los jesuitas en Bergara y el Real Seminario Patriótico Bascongado (Edificios, iglesia y propiedades)." In *II Seminario de Historia de la RSBP*, 257-271. Donostia: RSBAP, 1988.

Aragón Ruano, Álvaro and Alberto Angulo Morales. "Spanish Basque Country in Global Trade Networks in the Eighteenth Century." *International Journal of Maritime History* 25-1 (2013): 149-172.

Aragón Ruano, Álvaro and Xabier Alberdi Lonbide. "El premio de la plata y la devaluación del vellón en Guipúzcoa en el siglo XVII." *Cuadernos de Historia Moderna* 27 (2002): 131-167.

Aragón Ruano, Álvaro. "La evolución de la economía guipuzcoana en tiempos de Urdaneta: un período de desarrollo y expansión entre supuestas crisis." In *Andrés de Urdaneta: un hombre moderno*, edited by Susana Truchuelo García, 119-144. Ordizia: Ordiziako Udala, 2009.

_____. "La Guerra de la Convención, la separación de Guipúzcoa y los comerciantes vasco-franceses y bearneses." *Pedralbes. Revista d'historia moderna* 31 (2011): 167-232.

_____. ""... Faltar y ausentarse con esto los naturales de esta provinçia y quedar despoblada y hierma, sin defensa alguna...." Discursos de frontera en Gipuzkoa durante la Edad Moderna." In *Naciones en el Estado-Nación: la formación cultural y política de naciones en la Europa contemporánea*, edited by Joseba Agirreazkuenaga Zigorraga and Eduardo J. Alonso Olea, 401-410. Barcelona: Editorial Base, 2014.

_____. "Discursos de frontera en el Pirineo occidental durante la Edad Moderna." In *Una década prodigiosa. Beligerancia y negociación entre la Corona y las provincias vascas (1717-1728)*, edited by Álvaro Aragón Ruano and Alberto Angulo Morales, 155-174. Bilbao: UPV/EHU, 2019.

_____. "Euskal Herria «itsastarra» lehen mundubiraren testuinguruan." In *Elkano eta lehen mundubira: 500 urte geroago*, 75-102. Getaria: Mundubira 500 Elkano Fundazioa, 2020.

Aramburu-Zudaire, José Miguel. "América y los vascos en la Edad Moderna. Una perspectiva historiográfica." *Vasconia* 34 (2005): 249-274.

Aranzadi, Juan. *Milenarismo vasco. Edad de Oro, etnia y nativismo*. Madrid: Taurus, 2000.

Arcos Herrera, Carol. "Sujetos de controversia: aportes para una bibliografía sobre las mujeres en el siglo XVIII y la Ilustración." *Revista de Crítica Literaria Latinoamericana* 67 (2008): 111-122.

Ardash Bonialian, Mariano. *El Pacífico hispanoamericano: política y comercio asiático en el imperio español, 1680-1784*. México: El Colegio de México, 2012.

Aresti Esteban, Nerea. "Los argumentos de la exclusión. Mujeres y liberalismo en la España contemporánea." *Historia Constitucional* 13 (2012): 407-431.

Armitage, David. "Tres conceptos de historia atlántica." *Revista de Occidente* 281 (2004): 7-28.

Arpal Poblador, Jesús. La sociedad tradicional en el País Vasco: el estamento de los hidalgos en Guipúzcoa. San Sebastián: Haranburu, 1979.

Arretxea, Larraitz and Mikel Lertxundi. "El patronazgo del General Francisco de Echeveste." *Ondare* 19 (2000): 269-276.

_____. "Los retratos de los fundadores del Colegio de las Vizcaínas en México." *Ondare* 19 (2000): 437-442.

Artola, Miguel (Ed.). *Historia de Donostia San Sebastián*. Donostia: Nerea, 2000.

Astigarraga, Jesús. "Sociedades económicas y comercio privilegiado. La Sociedad Bascongada, La Compañía de Caracas y la vertiente marítima de la Ilustración vasca." *Itsas Memoria. Revista de Estudios Marítimos del País Vasco* 6 (2009): 669-688.

Atienza López, Ángela. ""No pueden ellos ver mejor...." Autonomía, autoridad y sororidad en el gobierno de los claustros femeninos en la Edad Moderna." *Arenal* 26-1 (2019): 5-34.

Auñamendi Eusko Entziklopedia. Eusko Ikaskuntza.

Ayerbe Iribar, Mª Rosa. "Manuel de Larramendi y la enseñanza femenina en el siglo XVIII. Constituciones del Seminario de niñas "Nuestra Señora de la Soledad," de Bergara (1741)." *Boletín de la RSBAP* 64-2 (2008): 797-801.

Azcona Pastor, José Manuel. *Possible Paradises. Basque Emigration to Latin America*. Reno: University of Nevada Press, 2002.

_____. Identidad y estructura de la emigración vasca y navarra hacia Iberoamérica (siglos XVI-XXI). Madrid: Thomson Reuters-Aranzadi, 2015.

Azpiazu Elorza, José Antonio. "Las escuelas en el País Vasco a principios de la Edad Moderna. El interés por la enseñanza por parte de las instituciones y particulares." *Vasconia* 27, (1998): 147-164.

_____. "Los guipuzcoanos y Sevilla en la Alta Edad Moderna." *Itsas Memoria. Revista de Estudios Marítimos del País Vasco* 4 (2003): 207-225.

Bagües i Erriondo, Jon. "El conde de Peñaflorida, impulsor de la Ilustración musical en el País Vasco." *Musiker, Cuadernos de Música* 4 (1988): 106-148.

Baldellou Monclús, Daniel and José Antonio Salas Auséns. "Noviazgo y matrimonio en Aragón. Casarse en la Europa del Antiguo Régimen." *Revista de Historia Moderna. Anales de la Universidad de Alicante* 34 (2016): 79-105.

Baldellou Monclús, Daniel. "Idiosincrasia del modelo de transmisión de la propiedad en el Antiguo Régimen: el modelo de las familias del Pirineo." *Actas del I Congreso Internacional Jóvenes Investigadores Siglo de Oro*, (2012): 11-21.

Baranda, Nieves. Cortejo a lo prohibido. Lectoras y escritoras en la España moderna. Madrid: Arco, 2005.

Barberá Heredia, Ester. "Perspectiva socio-cognitiva: estereotipos y esquemas de género." In *Psicología y género*, edited by Ester Barberá e Isabel Martínez Benlloch, 58-69. Madrid: Pearson Prentice Hall, 2004.

Barbieri, Elena and Rosa de Castro. "Ciudadanía y feminismo: categorías a debatir." In *Actas de las XIII Jornadas Rosarinas de Antropología Socio-cultural*, 1-10. Rosario: Universidad de Rosario, 2016.

Barrio Moya, José Luis. "La librería y otros bienes de Doña Ana María de Soroa, dama guipuzcoana del siglo XVIII (1743)." *Boletín de la RSBAP* 47-1-2 (1991): 163-180.

_____. "La biblioteca de Doña Luisa de Urrieta, dama donostiarra en el Madrid de Felipe V."

Boletín de la RSBAP 54-2 (1998): 435-445.

———. "La biblioteca de Doña Marcela Arteaga Arenaza y Tellechea, una dama bilbaína en el Madrid de Carlos IV (1805)." *Boletín de la RSBAP* 66-2 (2010): 639-651.

Benito Pascual, Jesús de. Mujer e instrucción pública. Origen del magisterio femenino en Guipúzcoa (1800-1833). Donostia: Gipuzkoako Foru Aldundia, Emakunde, 1999.

Berasategui Garaizábal, Luis. Biblioteca Alameda. La biblioteca de una familia ilustrada en Vitoria. Vitoria: Manuscrito, 2004.

Bisha, Robin, Jehanne M. Gheith, Christine Holden and William G. Wagner. *Russian Women. Experience & Expression. An Anthology of Sources.* Bloomington: Indiana University Press, 2002.

Blanco Mozo, Juan Luis. Orígenes y desarrollo de la Ilustración vasca en Madrid. De la Congregación de San Ignacio a la Sociedad Bascongada. Madrid: Real Sociedad Bascongada de los Amigos del País, 2011.

Bodelón, Encarna. "Feminismo y Derecho: mujeres que van más allá de lo jurídico." In *Género y dominación. Críticas feministas del derecho y el poder*, edited by Gemma Nicolás and Encarna Bodelón, 95-116. Barcelona: Anthropos, 2009.

Bolufer Peruga, Mónica. "Josefa Amar e Inés Joyes: dos perspectivas femeninas sobre el matrimonio en el siglo XVIII." In *Historia de la mujer e historia del matrimonio*, edited by María Victoria López-Cordón and Montserrat Carbonell Esteller, 203-217. Murcia: Universidad de Murcia, 1997.

———. In *Mujer y deseo: representaciones prácticas de vida*, edited by María José de la Pascua, María del Rosario García-Doncel and Gloria Espigado, 357-382. Cádiz: Universidad de Cádiz, 2004.

———. "De violentar las pasiones a educar el sentimiento: el matrimonio y la civilidad Dieciochesca." In *Actas de la XI Reunión Científica de la Fundación Española de Historia Moderna*, 349-360. Granada: Universidad de Granada, Volume 2, 2012.

———. "Modelar conductas y sensibilidades: un campo abierto de indagación histórica." In *Educar los sentimientos y las costumbres. Una mirada desde la historia*, edited by Mónica Bolufer, Carolina Blutrach and Juan Gomis, 7-17. Zaragoza: Institución Fernando el Católico, CSIC, 2014.

———. "Sociabilidad mixta y civilización: miradas desde España." In *Educar los sentimientos y las costumbres. Una mirada desde la historia*, edited by Mónica Bolufer, Carolina Blutrach and Juan Gomis, 149-173. Zaragoza: Institución Fernando el Católico, CSIC, 2014.

———. "En torno a la sensibilidad dieciochesca: discursos, prácticas, paradojas." In *Las mujeres y las emociones en Europa y América. Siglos XVII-XIX*, edited by María Luisa Candau Chacón, 29-56. Santander: Universidad de Cantabria, 2016.

———. "Afectos razonables: equilibrios de la sensibilidad dieciochesca." In *La cultura de las emociones y las emociones en la cultura española contemporánea (siglos XVIII-XXI)*, edited by Luisa Elena Delgado, Pura Fernández and Jo Labanyi, 35-56. Madrid: Cátedra, 2018.

———. Arte y artificio de la vida en común. Los modelos de comportamiento y sus tensiones en el siglo de las Luces. Madrid: Marcial Pons, 2019.

Borderías, Cristina. "El trabajo de las mujeres. Discursos y prácticas." In *Historia de las mujeres en España y América Latina*, edited by Isabel Morant, 353-380. Madrid: Cátedra, Volume 3, 2005.

Brading, David A. *Mineros y comerciantes en el México borbónico (1763-1810).* México D.F.:

Fondo de Cultura Económica, 2015.

Cantero Rosales, María Ángeles. "De "perfecta casada" a "ángel del hogar" o la construcción del arquetipo femenino en el XIX." *Revista Electrónica de Estudios Filológicos* 14 (2007).

Capel Martínez, Rosa María. "Mujer y educación en el Antiguo Régimen." *Historia de la Educación. Revista interuniversitaria* 26 (2007): 85-110.

———. "Preludio de una emancipación: la emergencia de la mujer ciudadana." *Cuadernos de Historia Moderna* 6 (2007): 155-179.

Cardozo Uzcátegui, Alejandro. "El lobby cisatlántico del cacao. La Real Compañía Guipuzcoana de Caracas y el poder vasco en la provincia de Venezuela." In *Recuperando el Norte. Empresas, capitales y proyectos atlánticos en la economía imperial hispánica*, edited by Alberto Angulo Morales and Álvaro Aragón Ruano, 195-216. Bilbao: UPV/EHU, 2016.

Carrera Stampa, Manuel. "El Colegio de las Vizcaínas. Primera escuela laica en el continente americano." *Memoria de la Academia mexicana de la Historia* 26-4 (1967): 403-443.

Cava Mesa, María Jesús. *Un paseo por la historia de Bilbao*. Bilbao: Universidad de Deusto, 2008.

Chaparro Sainz, Álvaro. "Del pupitre a la espada: el Real Seminario de Vergara, cantera de militares." *Revista de Demografía Histórica* 27 (2009): 55-82.

———. "La política educativa de las familias ilustradas vascas. La familia Álava y el Real Seminario de Vergara." In *Familias, jerarquización y movilidad social*, edited by Giovanni Levi and Raimundo E. Rodríguez Pérez, 71-86. Murcia: Universidad de Murcia, 2010.

———. Educarse para servir al rey. El Real Seminario de Vergara (1776-1804). Bilbao: UPV/EHU, 2011.

Chico Comerón, Cirilo. "La Guerra de la Convención en Guipúzcoa (1793-1795): daños causados por las tropas francesas." *Espacio, Tiempo y Forma, Serie IV, Historia Moderna* 24 (2011): 175-187.

Chipman, Donald E. *Spanish Texas, 1519-1821*. Austin: University of Texas Press, 1992.

Cierbide Martinena, Ricardo. "La Compañía Guipuzcoana de Caracas y los vascos en Venezuela durante el siglo XVIII." *Revista Internacional de Estudios Vascos* 42-1 (1997): 63-75.

Colección de documentos inéditos para la historia de Guipúzcoa. San Sebastián: Diputación de Guipúzcoa, 1965.

Craveri, Benedetta. "La contribución de las mujeres a una nueva forma de civilidad (ss. XVII-XVIII)." In *Educar los sentimientos y las costumbres. Una mirada desde la historia*, edited by Mónica Bolufer, Carolina Blutrach and Juan Gomis, 131-148. Zaragoza: Institución Fernando el Católico, CSIC, 2014.

Delgado Criado, Buenaventura. Historia de la educación en España y América. La educación en la España Moderna (siglos XVI-XVIII). Madrid: Fundación Santa María, 1993.

Delgado, Luisa Elena, Pura Fernández and Jo Labanyi. "Cartografía de las emociones en la cultura española contemporánea: teorías, prácticas y contextos culturales." In *La cultura de las emociones y las emociones en la cultura española contemporánea (siglos XVIII-XXI)*, edited by Luisa Elena Delgado, Pura Fernández and Jo Labanyi, 9-33. Madrid: Cátedra, 2018.

Díaz de Durana, José Ramón. "La hidalguía universal en el País Vasco. Tópicos sobre sus orígenes y causas de su desigual generalización." *Cuadernos de Alzate* 31 (2004): 49-64.

Echeberria Ayllón, Iker. "Breve aproximación a la autoridad femenina en el s. XVIII. El extraño caso de Gregoria de Urbina." *Sancho el Sabio. Revista de cultura e investigación vasca* 37 (2014): 33-52.

———. "Afectos olvidados." Mujeres de la élite vasca en el siglo XVIII. Tesis Doctoral, UPV/EHU, 2020.

Elliott, John H. *Imperios del mundo atlántico. España y Gran Bretaña en América, 1492-1830.* Madrid: Taurus, 2006.

———. *España, Europa y el mundo de ultramar (1500-1800).* Madrid: Taurus, 2010.

Erdozain Azpilikueta, Pilar and Fernando Mikelarena Peña. "Algunas consideraciones en torno a la investigación del régimen de herencia troncal en la Euskal Herria tradicional." *Vasconia* 28 (1991): 71-91.

Escamilla González, Francisco Iván. *Los intereses malentendidos. El Consulado de Comerciantes de México y la monarquía española, 1700-1739.* México: UNAM, 2011.

Fagoaga e Yragorri, Francisco de. *Tablas de las cuentas del valor líquido de la plata del diezmo y del intrínseco y natural de la que se llama quintada y de la reducción de sus leyes a la de 12 dineros.* México: Imprenta de José Bernardo de Hogal, 1729.

Fattaccia, Irene. "The Resilience and Boomerang Effect of Chocolate: A Product's Globalization and Commodification." In *Global Goods and the Spanish Empire, 1492-1824. Circulation, Resistance and Diversity*, edited by Bethany Aram and Bartolomé Yun-Casalilla, 255-273. London: Palgrave Macmillan, 2014.

Fernández González, Fernando. *Comerciantes vascos en Sevilla, 1650-1700.* Vitoria-Gasteiz: Diputación de Sevilla/Gobierno Vasco, 2000.

———. "Castilla, Sevilla y el País Vasco en la segunda mitad del siglo XVIII." *Itsas Memoria. Revista de Estudios Marítimos del País Vasco* 4 (2003): 287-295.

Foz y Foz, Pilar and Estela Mejía Restrepo. *Fuentes primarias para la historia de la educación de la mujer en Europa y América: archivos históricos de la Compañía de María Nuestra Señora, 1607-1921.* Roma: s.n., 1989.

Foz y Foz, Pilar. *La revolución pedagógica en la Nueva España (1754-1820).* Madrid: Instituto Gonzalo Fernández de Oviedo, Tomo I, 1981.

Franco Rubio, Gloria. "Nicolás Fernández de Moratín y El arte de las putas." In *Feminismo y misoginia en la literatura española. Fuentes literarias para la Historia de las Mujeres*, edited by Cristina Segura Graíño, 97-122. Madrid: Narcea, 2001.

———. "La contribución literaria de Moratín y otros hombres de letras al modelo de mujer doméstica." *Cuadernos de Historia Moderna* 6 (2007): 221-254.

Frasquet, Ivana. "Actrices en la independencia de México: buscando su lugar en la Historia." In *Jamás ha llovido reyes del cielo. De independencias, revoluciones y liberalismos en Iberoamérica*, edited by Ivana Frasquet, 209-222. Quito: Corporación Editorial Nacional, 2013.

Gabarain, María Teresa. "La influencia europea en la Ilustración del País Vasco. Presencia de jóvenes vascos en los colegios franceses durante el siglo XVIII." In *V Seminario de Historia de la RSBAP*, 743-754. Donostia-San Sebastián: RSBAP, 1996.

Gárate Ojanguren, Montserrat. "Las cuentas de la Real Compañía Guipuzcoana de Caracas." *Moneda y Crédito* 153 (1980): 49-75.

———. "El marqués de Narros y el comercio directo con América (utilidad y necesidad del comercio)." In *II Seminario de Historia de la RSBP*, 273-309. Donostia: RSBAP, 1988.

———. *La Real Compañía Guipuzcoana de Caracas.* San Sebastián: Sociedad Guipuzcoana de Ediciones y Publicaciones, 1990.

———. "Navarros y guipuzcoanos unidos en empresas económicas del siglo XVIII." *Revista Internacional de Estudios Vascos* 37-1 (1992): 25-42.

———. "Remesas de capitales mexicanos a Europa en el siglo XIX. La participación vasca." In *Los vascos en las regiones de México. Siglos XVI-XX*, edited by Amaya Garritz, 281-294.

México: UNAM, Tomo I, 1996.

García Fuentes, Lutgardo, *Los peruleros y el comercio de Sevilla con las Indias, 1580-1630*. Sevilla: Universidad de Sevilla, 1997.

——. "La crisis del siglo XVII y las remesas de caudales indianos desde Sevilla para el País Vasco." *Archivo hispalense. Revista histórica, literaria y artística* 84-255 (2001): 27-42.

——. "Los vascos en la Carrera de Indias en la Edad Moderna: una minoría dominante." *Temas Americanistas* 16 (2003): 29-49.

García López, Ana Belén. "La participación de las mujeres en la independencia hispanoamericana a través de los medios de comunicación." *Historia y Comunicación Social* 16 (2011): 33-49.

García Vallejo, María Cristina. "El Colegio de San Ignacio de Loyola ante la extinción de la cofradía de Nuestra Señora de Aránzazu, 1861." In *Los vascos en las regiones de México. Siglos XVI-XX*, edited by Amaya Garritz, 239-256. México: UNAM, Tomo II, 1996.

García, Clara. "Sociedad, crédito y cofradía en la Nueva España a fines de la época colonial: el caso de Nuestra Señora de Aránzazu." *Historias. Revista de la dirección de estudios históricos del Instituto Nacional de Antropología e Historia* 3 (1983): 53-68.

García-Abásolo, Antonio, "Cofradías y hospitales de Filipinas (siglos XVI-XVIII)." In *Devoción, paisanaje e identidad. Las cofradías y congregaciones de naturales en España y en América (siglos XVI-XIX)*, edited by Óscar Álvarez Gila, Alberto Angulo Morales and Jon Ander Ramos Martínez, 57-80. Bilbao: UPV/EHU, 2014.

García-Ayluardo, Clara. "El milagro de la Virgen. El desarrollo de los vascos como grupo de poder en la Nueva España." In *IV Seminario de Historia de la Real Sociedad Bascongada de los Amigos del País. "La RSBAP y Méjico,"* 439-457. Donostia-San Sebastián: RSBAP, Tomo I, 1993.

Garmendia Arruebarrena, José. "La Real Compañía Guipuzcoana de Caracas y su contribución en Sevilla." *Cuadernos de Sección, Eusko Ikaskuntza, Sociedad de Estudios Vascos* 8 (1986): 48-58.

——. *Cádiz, los vascos y la carrera de Indias*. San Sebastián: Eusko Ikaskuntza, 1989.

Gómez Murillo, Ana Guillermina. "Análisis de redes sociales en los negocios ganaderos de los condes de San Mateo del Valparaíso y marqueses de Jaral de Berrio. Siglo XVIII." In *Historia y patrimonio cultural*, edited by Manuel Alcántara, Mercedes García Montero y Francisco Sánchez López, 1011-1023. Salamanca: Universidad de Salamanca, 2018.

González Dios, Estíbaliz. "Gipuzkoa en la primera globalización (ss. XVI-XVIII)." In *Síntesis de la Historia de Gipuzkoa*, edited by Álvaro Aragón Ruano e Iker Echeberria Ayllón, 269-362. Donostia: Diputación Foral de Gipuzkoa, 2017.

Gorosabel, Pablo de. Diccionario histórico-geográfico-descriptivo de los pueblos, valles, partidos, alcaldías y uniones de Guipúzcoa. Tolosa: Imprenta de Pedro Gurruchaga, 1862.

Hausberger, Bernd. "La guerra de los vicuñas contra los vascongados en Potosí y la etnización de los vascos a principios de la Edad Moderna." In *Excluir para ser. Procesos identitarios y fronteras sociales en la América hispánica (siglos XVII-XVIII)*, edited by Christian Büschges and Frédérique Langue, 23-58. Madrid: Iberoamericana, 2005.

Héctor Trejo Huerta, Jesús. "Don Ambrosio de Meave y el paisanaje, lealtad y asistencialismo entre dos instituciones vascas." *Euskonews* (2011).

Herzog, Tamar. "Private Organizations as Global Networks in Early Modern Spain and Spanish America." In *The Collective and the Public in Latin America: Cultural Identities and Political Order*, edited by Luis Roniger and Tamar Herzog, 117-133. (Brighton: Sussex Academic Press, 2000), 117-133

Imízcoz Beunza, José María (Ed.). Casa, familia y sociedad (País Vasco, España y América, siglos XV-XIX). Leioa: UPV/EHU, 2004.

Imízcoz Beunza, José María and Rafael Guerrero. "Familias en la Monarquía. La política familiar de las elites vascas y navarras en el Imperio de los Borbones." In *Casa, familia y sociedad*, edited by José María Imízcoz Beunza, 177-238. Bilbao: UPV/EHU, 2004.

Intxaustegi Jauregi, Nere Jone. *La mujer religiosa en Bizkaia durante los siglos XVI-XVIII*. Bilbao: Diputación Foral de Bizkaia, 2018.

Iriarte, Joaquín. "Javier María de Munibe e Idiáquez. Conde de Peñaflorida. Fundador de la Real Sociedad Bascongada de los Amigos del País." *Boletín de la RSBAP* 22-2 (1966): 191-214.

Jiménez Codinach, Guadalupe. "Algunos miembros de la Real Sociedad Bascongada y sus descendientes, amigos de la Independencia de la Nueva España." In *IV Seminario de Historia de la Real Sociedad Bascongada de los Amigos del País*. "*La RSBAP y Méjico,*" 841-869. Donostia-San Sebastián: RSBAP, Tomo 2, 1993.

Johnson, Robert and Maite Zubiaurre. *Antropología del pensamiento feminista español*. Madrid: Cátedra, 2012.

Kintana Goirienea, Jurgi. "La "nación vascongada" y sus luchas en el Potosí del siglo XVII. Fuentes de estudio y estado de la cuestión." *Anuario de Estudios Americanos* 59-1 (2002): 287-310.

La Real Sociedad Bascongada y América. Madrid: Fundación BBVA, 1992.

Ladd, Doris M. La nobleza mexicana en la época de la independencia, 1780-1826. México: Fondo de Cultura Económica, 1984.

Langer, Johnni. "O mito do Eldorado: origem e significado no imaginário sul-americano (século XVI)." *Revista de História* 136 (1997): 25-40.

Langue, Frédérique. Los señores de Zacatecas. Una aristocracia minera del siglo XVIII novohispano. México: Fondo de Cultura Económica, 1999.

Laspalas Pérez, Javier. "La legislación sobre escuelas de primeras letras y su administración en Navarra durante la segunda mitad del siglo XVIII." *Educación XXI* 5 (2002): 199-226.

Lema Pueyo, José Ángel. "De "Ipuzkoa" a la hermandad de villas de Gipuzkoa (ss. VI-VX)." In *Síntesis de la Historia de Gipuzkoa*, edited by Álvaro Aragón Ruano e Iker Echeberria Ayllón, 195-268. Donostia: Diputación Foral de Gipuzkoa, 2017.

León Fray, Luis de. *La perfecta casada*. Salamanca: Tomás de Alva librero, 1603.

López Atxurra, Rafael. "Historia de las instituciones educativas en Euskal Herria. La enseñanza primaria en el Antiguo Régimen. Pautas para la investigación." In *Haciendo Historia. Homenaje a Mª Ángeles Larrea*, edited by Rafael Mieza and Juan Gracia, 419-445. Bilbao: UPV/EHU, 2004.

López Céspedes, José Jesús. "Novela del siglo XVIII y construcción de la sentimentalidad ilustrada en España. "Voz de la naturaleza" de I. García Malo." In *El mundo hispánico en el Siglo de las Luces*, 831-842. Madrid: Universidad Complutense de Madrid, Volume 2, 1996.

López-Cordón, María Victoria. *Condición femenina y razón ilustrada. Josefa Amar y Borbón*. Zaragoza: Universidad de Zaragoza, 2006.

Los vascos y América. Actas de las Jornadas sobre el comercio vasco con América en el siglo XVIII y la Real Compañía Guipuzcoana de Caracas en el II centenario de Carlos II. Bilbao: Fundación Banco de Vizcaya, 1980.

Lougee, Carolyn C. ""Its Frequent Visitor." Death at Boarding School in Early Modern Europe." In *Women's Education in Early Modern Europe. A History, 1500-1800*, edited by Barbara J. Whitehead, 193-224. New York: Garland Publishing, 1999.

Ludlow Wiechers, Leonor. "Los vascos-mexicanos ante los gobiernos independientes. Relaciones financieras y políticas." In *IV Seminario de Historia de la Real Sociedad Bascongada de los Amigos del País. "La RSBAP y Méjico,"* 905-924. Donostia-San Sebastián: RSBAP, Tomo I, 1993.

Luque Alcaide, Elisa. "Autonomía jurídica del Colegio de las Vizcaínas en el siglo XVIII (estudio de unos documentos romanos)." *Anuario Mexicano de Historia del Derecho* 2 (1990): 151-167.

_____. "El colegio de las vizcaínas, iniciativa vasco-navarra para la educación de la mujer en la Nueva España en el siglo XVIII." In *X Simposio Internacional de Teología de la Universidad de Navarra*, 1443-1454. Pamplona: Universidad de Navarra, Tomo II, 1990.

_____. "Investigaciones sobre la Cofradía de Aránzazu de México (siglos XVII-XIX)." *Anuario de la historia de la Iglesia* 2 (1993): 303-306.

_____. "Relaciones intercontinentales de la Cofradía de Aránzazu de México." In *IV Seminario de Historia de la Real Sociedad Bascongada de los Amigos del País. "La RSBAP y Méjico,"* 459-481. Donostia-San Sebastián: RSBAP, Tomo I, 1993.

_____. "Asociacionismo vasco en la Nueva España: modelo étnico-cultural." In *Los vascos en las regiones de México. Siglos XVI-XX*, edited by Amaya Garritz, 67-86. México: UNAM, Tomo II, 1996.

_____. "Recursos de la Cofradía de Aránzazu de México ante la corona (1729-1763)." *Revista de Indias* 56-206 (1996): 205-219.

_____. "La cofradía de Aránzazu de México (1681-1861). Continuidad de un proyecto." In *Devoción, paisanaje e identidad. Las cofradías y congregaciones de naturales en España y en América (siglos XVI-XIX)*, edited by Óscar Álvarez Gila, Alberto Angulo Morales and Jon Ander Ramos Martínez, 227-246. Bilbao: UPV/EHU, 2014.

Madariaga Orbea, Juan and Javier Esteban Ochoa de Eribe. "Experiencias divergentes, lecturas diferenciales. Los propietarios de bibliotecas particulares de Guipúzcoa (1675-1849)." *Historia social* 89 (2017): 139-156.

Madariaga Orbea, Juan. *Sociedad y lengua vasca en los siglos XVII y XVIII*. Bilbao: Eukaltzaindia, 2014.

Manzanos Arreal, Paloma and Francisca Vives Casas. *Las mujeres en Vitoria-Gasteiz a lo largo de los siglos. Recorridos y biografías*. Vitoria-Gasteiz: Ayuntamiento de Vitoria-Gasteiz, 2001.

Mary Trojani, Cécile. "La amistad en el Siglo de las Luces. La Real Sociedad Bascongada en las fuentes epistolares." *Boletín de la RSBAP* 60-2 (2004): 609-628.

_____. "Aproximación semántica a un epistolario. Los tratamientos en la correspondencia entre Peñaflorida y Pedro Jacinto de Álava." In *La carta como fuente y como texto. Las correspondencias societarias del siglo XVIII: La Real Sociedad Bascongada de los Amigos del País*, edited by José María Urquía Echave and Antonio Risco, 239-254. Donostia: RSBAP, 2005.

_____. "Le Collège Patriotique de Vergara et les Amis de la *Bascongada* en Amérique." In *Amitiés. Le cas des mondes américains*, edited by La Promenade, 31-44. Tensions 1, 2012.

Mata Montes de Oca, María Cristina. "Mujeres en el límite del periodo virreinal." In *Historia de las mujeres en México*, 47-67. México: Instituto Nacional de Estudios Históricos de las Revoluciones de México, 2015.

McClelland, Averil E. *The education of women in the United States*. New York: Gerland Publishing, 1992.

Medina Doménech, Rosa María. "Sentir la Historia. Propuestas para una agenda de investigación feminista en la historia de las emociones." *Arenal* 19-1 (2012): 161-199.

Méndez Reyes, Salvador. "Los Fagoaga: magnates de las minas Zacatecanas y de la Independencia." In *Los vascos en las regiones de México. Siglos XVI-XX*, edited by Amaya Garritz, 297-308. México: UNAM, Tomo V, 1999.

Mikelarena Peña, Fernando. "La biblioteca de Pedro Miguel de Ligués, comerciante de lanas de Cintruénigo." *Sancho el Sabio* 23 (2005): 63-88.

———. "La biblioteca de un notable rural. La colección de don Francisco de Echarren y Atondo, hacendado de Valtierra." *Príncipe de Viana* 65 (2004): 917-945.

———. "La cultura libraria en la Navarra rural entre 1750 y 1849." *Historia Contemporánea* 34 (2007): 283-322.

———. "El final de una biblioteca centenaria. La historia de la Biblioteca de la Real Sociedad Tudelana de los Deseosos del Bien Público." *Revista Internacional de Estudios Vascos* 53-1 (2008): 183-215.

———. "La biblioteca de Francisco Javier Vidarte y Mendinueta, un liberal navarro." *Bulletin Hispanique* 110-2 (2008): 449-485.

———. "Los libros de historia de la biblioteca de Juan Antonio Fernández, erudito tudelano y académico correspondiente de la RAH." *Príncipe de Viana* 69 (2008): 459-495.

Molière. *Las preciosas ridículas*. Madrid: Cátedra, 2000.

Morant Deusa, Isabel and Mónica Bolufer Peruga, Amor, matrimonio y familia. La construcción histórica de la familia moderna. Madrid: Síntesis, 1998.

Morant Deusa, Isabel. "¿Qué es una mujer? O la condición sentimental de la mujer." In *Mujeres en la historia del pensamiento*, edited by Rosa María Rodríguez Magda, 145-165. Barcelona: Anthropos, 1997.

———. "Mujeres ilustradas en el debate de la educación. Francia y España." *Cuadernos de Historia Moderna* III, Anejos (2004): 59-84.

———. "El hombre y la mujer en el matrimonio. Moral y sentimientos familiares." In *Familia y organización social en Europa y América, siglos XV-XX*, edited by Francisco Chacón Jiménez, Juan Hernández Franco and Francisco García González, 185-209. Murcia: Universidad de Murcia, 2007.

———. "Las costumbres del amor y la diferencia de sexos en la novela de la modernidad." In *Las huellas de Foucault en la historiografía. Poderes, cuerpos y deseos*, edited by Henar Gallego Franco e Isabel del Val Valdivieso, 135-162. Barcelona: Icaria, 2013.

———. "Educar deleitando. Los usos de la novela formativa en el siglo XVIII." In *El siglo XVIII en femenino. Las mujeres en el Siglo de las Luces*, edited by Manuel-Reyes García Hurtado, 277-292. Madrid: Síntesis, 2016.

Moreno Almárcegui, José Antonio and Ana Zabalza Seguín. El origen histórico de un sistema de heredero único. El prepirineo navarro, 1540-1739. Pamplona: Rialp, 1999.

Munibe, Xabier María de. "Historia de la Real Sociedad Bascongada." *Revista Internacional de Estudios Vascos* 22 (1931): 443-482.

Muriel, Josefina. "Las instituciones educativas de los vascos para mujeres de México. Época Colonial." In *IV Seminario de Historia de la Real Sociedad Bascongada de los Amigos del País. "La RSBAP y Méjico,"* 316-423. Donostia-San Sebastián: RSBAP, Volume I, 1993.

———. "De Isabel de Urdiñola a María Ignacia de Azlor y Echevers." In *Los vascos en las regiones de México. Siglos XVI-XX*, edited by Amaya Garritz, 153-164. México: UNAM, Tomo III, 1997.

———. "Los arzobispos vascos y sus obras dedicadas a las mujeres novohispanas." In *Los vascos en las regiones de México. Siglos XVI-XX*, edited by Amaya Garritz, 55-72. México: UNAM,

Tomo IV, 1999.

_____. "La música en las instituciones femeninas existente en el Archivo Histórico del Colegio de San Ignacio de Loyola, Vizcaínas." In *Una Mujer, Un Legado, Una Historia: Homenaje a Josefina Muriel*, 221-226. México: Universidad Autónoma de México, 2000.

_____. La sociedad novohispana y sus colegios de niñas. Tomo II. Fundaciones del siglo XVII y XVIII. México D.F.: UNAM, 2004.

Nash, Margaret A. "Young Ladies' Academy of Philadelphia." In *Historical Dictionary of Women's Education in the United States*, edited by Linda Eisenmann, 498-499. Westport: Greenwood Press, 1998.

_____. Women's Education in the United States. 1780-1840. New York: Palgrave McMillan, 2005.

Notitia Vasconiae. Historiadores, juristas y pensadores políticos de Vasconia. Antigüedad, Edad Media y Moderna. Madrid: Fundación Iura Vasconiae, Marcial Pons, 2019.

Obregón, Gonzalo. *El Real Colegio de San Ignacio de México (Las Vizcaínas)*. Ciudad de México: El Colegio de México, 1949.

Odriozola Oyarbide, María Lourdes and María Montserrat Gárate Ojanguren. "Emigración y remesas de capitales. Siglos XVIII-XIX." In *Los movimientos migratorios en la construcción de las sociedades modernas*, edited by Karmele Zarraga Sangroniz and Manuel González Portilla, 471-488. Bilbao: UPV/EHU, 1996.

Olabarria y Ferrari, Enrique de. El Real Colegio de San Ignacio de Loyola, vulgarmente Colegio de las Vizcaínas, en la actualidad Colegio de la Paz. México: Imprenta de Francisco Díaz de León, 1889.

Ortega Berruguete, Arturo Rafael. "Matrimonio, fecundidad y familia en el País Vasco a fines de la Edad Moderna." *Revista de Demografía Histórica* 7-1 (1989): 47-74.

Ortega López, Margarita. "La educación de la mujer en la Ilustración española." *Revista de educación* extra 1 (1988): 303-325.

Otazu, Alfonso de, and José Ramón Díaz de Durana. *El espíritu emprendedor de los vascos*. Madrid: Sílex, 2008.

Palacio Montiel, Celia. "La participación femenina en la Independencia de México." In *Historia de las mujeres en México*, 69-92. México: Instituto Nacional de Estudios Históricos de las Revoluciones de México, 2015.

Palacios Fernández, Emilio. "Samaniego y la educación en la Sociedad Bascongada de Amigos del País." In *I Seminario de historia de la Real Sociedad Bascongada de los Amigos del País*, 283-309. San Sebastián: RSBAP, 1986.

_____. "Proyección de la ilustración vasca en América." *Revista Internacional de Estudios Vascos* 43 (1998): 33-60.

_____. La mujer y las letras en la España del siglo XVIII. Madrid: Laberinto, 2002.

Panera Rico, Carmen María. "La edad de la Ilustración en España. Lazos de fortuna, devoción y saber entre el País Vasco y América." *Itsas Memoria. Revista de Estudios Marítimos del País Vasco* 3 (2000): 711-727.

Pascua Sánchez, María José de la. "Una aproximación a la Historia de la familia como espacio de afectos y desafectos: el mundo hispánico del Setecientos." *Chronica Nova* 27 (2000): 131-166.

Pellegrin, Nicole. "Las costureras de la historia: mujeres y trabajo en el Antiguo Régimen. Un balance historiográfico." *Arenal* 1-1 (1994): 25-38.

Perdices de Blas, Luis. *Pablo de Olavide (1725-1803), el ilustrado*. Madrid: Universidad Complutense, 1993.

———. "Mujer, educación y mercado de trabajo en el proyecto reformista de Pablo de Olavide." *ICE: Revista de Economía* 852 (2010): 99-111.

Pérez Herrero, Pedro. Plata y libranzas. La articulación comercial del México borbónico. México: El Colegio de México, 1988.

Pérez Rosales, Laura. *Familia, poder, riqueza y subversión: los Fagoaga novohispanos 1730-1830.* México: Universidad Iberoamericana, RSBAP, 2003.

Pérez Samper, María de los Ángeles. "Espacios y prácticas de sociabilidad en el siglo XVIII: tertulias, refrescos y cafés de Barcelona." *Cuadernos de Historia Moderna* 26 (2001): 11-55.

Pérez San Vicente, Guadalupe. Análisis Paleográfico sobre el Acta de Independencia. México: UNAM, 1961.

Pérez-Fuentes Hernández, Pilar. "Ganadores de pan" y "amas de casa." Otra mirada sobre la industrialización vasca. Bilbao: UPV/EHU, 2004.

Pescador, Juan Javier. "La familia Fagoaga y los matrimonios en la ciudad de México en el siglo XVIII." In *Familias Novohispanas. Siglos XVI al XIX*, edited by Pilar Gonzalbo Aizpuru, 203-226. México D.F.: El Colegio de México, 1991.

———. Familias y fortunas del Oiartzun antiguo. Microhistoria y genealogía, siglos XVI-XVIII. Oiartzun: Oiartzungo Udala, 1995.

———. "The New World inside a Basque villaje: the Oiartzun Valley and its Atlantic exchanges, 1550-1800." PhD diss., University of Michigan, 1998.

Porres Marijuán, Rosario. "Los protocolos notariales e Historia de la cultura. La biblioteca de don Diego Manuel de Esquivel y Verástegui." In *Aproximación metodológica a los protocolos notariales de Álava (Edad Moderna)*, edited by Rosario Porres Marijuán, 327-344. Bilbao: UPV/EHU, 1996.

Prada Camín, Fernanda. *Ocho siglos de historia de las clarisas en* España. Murcia: Editorial Espigas, 2013.

Quevedo, Francisco de. *La culta latiniparla*. Biblioteca Virtual Miguel de Cervantes.

Ramiro Moya, Francisco. *Mujeres y trabajo en la Zaragoza del siglo XVIII*. Zaragoza: Prensas universitarias de Zaragoza, 2012.

Ramos y Ramos, Pedro and Magdalena Rius de la Pola. "Tres momentos en la vida del Colegio de las Vizcaínas." In *Los vascos en las regiones de México. Siglos XVI-XX*, edited by Amaya Garritz, 103-116. México: UNAM, Tomo IV, 1999.

Recarte Barriola, Maite. "Ideario pedagógico de la Real Sociedad Bascongada de los Amigos del País, según los discursos de sus Juntas Generales." In *I Seminario de historia de la Real Sociedad Bascongada de los Amigos del País*, 311-322. San Sebastián: RSBAP, 1986.

Recarte Barriola, Maite. "La renovación educativa de la Ilustración vasca: la Real Sociedad Bascongada de los Amigos del País." *Revista Internacional de los Estudios Vascos* 37-2 (1992): 315-330.

Recarte Barriola, María Teresa. *Ilustración vasca y renovación educativa. La Real Sociedad Bascongada de los Amigos del País*. Salamanca: Universidad Pontificia de Salamanca, RSBAP, 1990.

Rey Castelao, Ofelia. "Las experiencias cotidianas de la lectura y la escritura en el ámbito femenino." In *Vida cotidiana en la España de la Ilustración*, edited by Inmaculada Arias de Saavedra, 615-644. Granada: Universidad de Granada, 2012.

———. "El trabajo de las mujeres rurales en la España moderna: un balance historiográfico (1994-2013)." *Revista de historiografía* 23-1 (2015): 183-210.

_____. "Libros y lecturas en la España de Carlos II." E-Spania. Revue interdisciplinaire d'etudes hispaniques médiévales et modernes 29 (2018).

Ríus de la Pola, Magdalena and Pedro Ramos y Ramos. "El Colegio de las Vizcaínas: una institución vasca en México a través de los siglos." In *Los vascos en las regiones de México. Siglos XVI-XX*, edited by Amaya Garritz, 165-173. México: UNAM, Tomo III, 1997.

Rivera, Manuel. *Los gobernantes de México*. México: Imprenta de J. M. Aguilar Ortiz, Tomo I, 1872.

Rodríguez Mirabal, Adelina. "La España reformista de comienzos del siglo XVIII y la nueva orientación del comercio ultramarino (El caso de la Compañía Guipuzcoana de Caracas)." *Ensayos Históricos. Anuario del Instituto de Estudios Hispánicos* 13 (2001): 39-54.

Rodriguez-San Pedro Bezares, Luis Enrique. Sensibilidades religiosas del Barroco: Carmelitas descalzas en San Sebastián. San Sebastián: Kutxa, 1990.

_____. "Claustros femeninos en la Ilustración: las carmelitas descalzas de San Sebastián." *Boletín de la RSBAP* 64-2 (2008): 771-794.

Roquero Ussía, María Rosario. "El convento y la política matrimonial de la burguesía donostiarra." *Boletín de Estudios Históricos de San Sebastián* 47 (2014): 119-145.

Rosain Unda, Gorka. "La Cofradía de Nuestra Señora de Aránzazu y los benefactores Aldaco, Echeveste y Meave. Colegio de las Vizcaínas." *Euskonews* (2004).

Ruiz Barrionuevo, Carmen. "Libros, lectura, enseñanza y mujeres en el siglo XVIII novohispano." *Revista de Filología* 25 (2007): 539-547.

_____. "Educación, libro y lectura en el siglo XVIII hispanoamericano." *América sin nombre* 18 (2013): 136-148.

Ruiz de Gordejuela Urquijo, Jesús. Vivir y morir en México. Vida cotidiana en el epistolario de los españoles vasconavarros 1750-1900. San Sebastián: Nuevos Aires, 2011.

_____. *Vasconavarros en México*. Ciudad de México: LID, 2012.

_____. "Los vascos y navarros en México en el tránsito de la colonia a la nación, 1800-1850." In *Del espacio cantábrico al mundo americano. Perspectivas sobre migración, etnicidad y retorno*, edited by Óscar Álvarez Gila and Juan Bosco Amores Carredano, 249-263. Bilbao: UPV/EHU, 2015.

Saladino García, Alberto. "La Real Sociedad Bascongada de los Amigos del País y las publicaciones periódicas del siglo XVIII en Nueva España." In *IV Seminario de Historia de la Real Sociedad Bascongada de los Amigos del País. "La RSBAP y Méjico,"* 729-736 (Donostia-San Sebastián: RSBAP, Tomo 2, 1993.

Samaniego, Félix María de [editing by Emilio Palacios Fernández]. *El jardín de Venus y otros jardines de verde hierba*. Madrid: Ediciones Siro, 1976.

Sánchez de Madariaga, Elena. "Caridad, devoción e identidad de origen: las cofradías de naturales y nacionales en el Madrid de la Edad Moderna." In *Devoción, paisanaje e identidad. Las cofradías y congregaciones de naturales en España y en América (siglos XVI-XIX)*, edited by Óscar Álvarez Gila, Alberto Angulo Morales and Jon Ander Ramos Martínez, 17-32. Bilbao: UPV/EHU, 2014.

Sánchez Erauskin, Miren. "Plan y ordenanzas de un seminario o casa de educación de señoritas. El proyecto de la Real Sociedad Bascongada de los Amigos del País." In *I Seminario de historia de la Real Sociedad Bascongada de los Amigos del País*, 323-348. San Sebastián: RSBAP, 1986.

Sanchiz Ruiz, Javier. "La familia Fagoaga. Apuntes genealógicos." *Estudios de historia novohispana* 23 (2000): 129-169.

Silván López-Almoguera, Leandro. "La Real Sociedad Bascongada de Amigos del País y el Real Seminario Patriótico Bascongado de Bergara." In *Historia del País Vasco—siglo XVIII-*, 175-190. Bilbao: Universidad de Deusto, 1985.

Sullivan, Constance A. "Las escritoras del siglo XVIII." In *Breve historia feminista de la literatura española (en lengua castellana)*, edited by Iris M. Zavala, 305-330. Barcelona: Anthropos, Tomo IV, 1997.

Taracena, María Pía. "La migración dorada: una familia vizcaína encuentra fama y fortuna en la ciudad de México a finales del siglo XVIII y siglo XIX. El caso de los Bassoco." In *Los vascos en las regiones de México. Siglos XVI-XX*, edited by Amaya Garritz, 217-229. México: UNAM, Tomo IV, 1999.

Tellechea Idígoras, José Ignacio. *La Ilustración vasca. Cartas de Xabier de Munibe, Conde de Peñaflorida, a Pedro Jacinto de Álava.* Vitoria-Gasteiz: Eusko Legebiltzarra-Parlamento Vasco, 1987.

_____. "Socios de la Real Sociedad Bascongada de los Amigos del País en México en el siglo XVIII." In *II Seminario de Historia de la RSBP*, 119-170. Donostia: RSBAP, 1988.

_____. El Colegio de las Vizcaínas de México y el Real Seminario de Vergara. Vitoria-Gasteiz: Eusko Jaurlaritza-Gobierno Vasco, 1992.

_____. "La Cofradía de Nuestra Señora de Aránzazu en la ciudad de México (1681-1794)." In *Las huellas de Aránzazu en América*, edited by Óscar Álvarez Gila e Idoia Arrieta Elizalde, 43-54. Donostia: Lankidetzan, 2004.

Torales Pacheco, María Cristina. "Los socios de la Real Sociedad Bascongada de los Amigos del País en México." In *IV Seminario de Historia de la Real Sociedad Bascongada de los Amigos del País. "La RSBAP y Méjico,"* 81-116. San Sebastián: RSBAP, Tomo I, 1993.

_____. "Presencia en México de los socios europeos de la RSBAP." In *La Bascongada y Europa. Actas del V Seminario de Historia de la Real Sociedad Bascongada de los Amigos del País*, edited by Guadalupe Rubio de Urquía and María Montserrat Gárate Ojanguren, 441-462. Donostia-San Sebastián: RSBAP, 1999.

_____. Ilustrados en la Nueva España. Los socios de la Real Sociedad Bascongada de los Amigos del País. México: Universidad Iberoamericana, 2001.

Turiso Sebastián, Jesús. "Entre el matrimonio y el celibato. Opciones vitales de la mujer de la élite limeña del siglo XVIII." In *VIII Congreso Internacional de Historia de América*, edited by Francisco Morales Padrón, 1364-1379. Gran Canaria: Cabildo de Gran Canaria, 2000.

_____. "Las claves de la armonía social. Matrimonio, patria potestad y dotes en la América virreinal." In *Dote matrimonial y redes de poder en el Antiguo Régimen en España e Hispanoamérica*, edited by Nora L. Siegrist de Gentile, and Edda O. Samudio, 197-216. Mérida: Universidad de los Andes, 2006.

_____. "Emigración, comerciantes y comercio en la región de Veracruz entre 1778-1822." *Naveg@mérica* 22 (2019): 1-25.

Urra Olazabal, Manuela. *La Compañía de María en Bergara. Dos siglos de Historia.* Vitoria-Gasteiz: Gobierno Vasco, 1999.

_____. La educación de la mujer y la Compañía de María en el País Vasco. Siglos XVIII y XIX. Orden de la Compañía de María Nuestra Señora: Ediciones Lestonnac, 2016.

Usunáriz Garayoa, Jesús María. "Un aspecto de la emigración navarra al Nuevo Mundo durante el siglo XVIII: las remesas indianas." *Príncipe de Viana* 13 (1991): 383-392.

Vaca de Osma, José Antonio. *Los vascos en la historia de España.* Madrid: Rialp, 1995.

Valero de García Lascuráin, Ana Rita, Baltazar Brito Gaudarrama and Juan Carlos Franco Montes de Oca, *Don Francisco de Echeveste. Armas y nobleza*. México D.F.: Secretaría de Educación Pública, Instituto Nacional de Antropología e Historia, Colegio de San Ignacio de Loyola, 2015.

Valle Pavón, Guillermina del. Mercaderes, comercio y consulados de Nueva España en el siglo XVIII. México: Instituto Mora, 2003.

_____. "En torno a los mercaderes de la ciudad de México y el comercio de Nueva España. Aportaciones a la bibliografía de la monarquía hispana en el periodo 1670-1740." In *Los virreinatos de Nueva España y del Perú (1680-1740). Un balance historiográfico*, edited by Bernard Lavallé, 135-150. Madrid: Casa de Velázquez, 2019.

Valverde Lamsfús, Lola. "La influencia del sistema de transmisión de la herencia sobre la condición de las mujeres en el País Vasco en la Edad Moderna." *Bilduma* 5 (1991): 123-135.

Velázquez Gutiérrez, María Elisa. *Mujeres de origen africano en la capital novohispana, siglos XVII y XVIII*. México D.F.: Instituto Nacional de Antropología e Historia, UNAM, 2006.

Vergara Iraeta, Ana Isabel. "Sexo e Identidad de Género: Diferencias en el Conocimiento Social de las Emociones y en el Modo de Compartirlas." Tesis doctoral, UPV/EHU, 1992.

Vidal Abarca y López, Juan. "La nobleza titulada en la Real Sociedad Bascongada de los Amigos del País." In *II Seminario de Historia de la RSBP*, 445-592. Donostia: RSBAP, 1988.

Viejo Yharrassarry, Tomás. "La segunda dote." *Vasconia* 8 (1986): 32-46.

Viñao Frago, Antonio. "La influencia de Campomanes, Olavide y Cabarrús en la educación." In *Historia de la educación en España y América*, edited by Buenaventura Delgado Criado, 657-668. Madrid: Morata, Volume II, 1993.

Vivas Pineda, Gerardo. "La Compañía Guipuzcoana de Caracas: los buques y sus hombres." In Los vascos y América. Actas de las Jornadas sobre el comercio vasco con América en el siglo XVIII y la Real Compañía Guipuzcoana de Caracas en el II centenario de Carlos II, 307-358. Bilbao: Fundación Banco de Vizcaya, 1980.

_____. La aventura naval de la Compañía Guipuzcoana de Caracas. Caracas: Fundación Polar, 1998.

Vives Almandoz, Gabriela, "La correspondencia de Miguel José de Olaso Zumalabe (1718-1773), primer secretario perpetuo de la Real Sociedad Bascongada de los Amigos del País." In *II Seminario de Historia de la RSBP*, 197-220. Donostia: RSBAP, 1988.

Vives, Juan Luis. *La formación de la mujer cristiana*. Valencia: Ayuntamiento de Valencia, 1994.

Yuste, Carmen. "Obras pías en Manila. La hermandad de la Santa Misericordia y las correspondencias a riesgo de mar en el tráfico transpacífico en el siglo XVIII." In *La Iglesia y sus bienes. De la amortización a la nacionalización*, edited by María del Pilar Martínez López-Cano, Elisa Speckman Guerra and Elisa Von Wobeser, 181-202. México D.F.: IIH-UNAM, 2004.

Zabalza Seguín, Ana. "El heredero ideal: prácticas sucesorias en la Navarra pirenaica durante la Edad Moderna (1550-1725)." In *Actas del Congreso Internacional de la Población: V Congreso de la ADEH*, edited by David Sven Reher Sullivan, 239-250. Logroño: 1999.

Zárate Toscano, Verónica. "Estrategias familiares de los nobles de origen vasco en la Nueva España." In *Los vascos en las regiones de México. Siglos XVI-XX*, edited by Amaya Garritz, 223-237. México: UNAM, Tomo II, 1999.

Zoraida Vázquez, Josefina. "La educación de la mujer en México en los siglos XVIII y XIX." *Diálogos: Artes, Letras, Ciencias Humanas* 17 (1981): 10-16.

INDEX

Note: Tables are indicated by t following the page number. End note information is indicated by n and note number following the page number.

Ágreda, María Jesús de, 11
Aguirrebengoa family, 74–75
Alamán, Lucas, 76–77
Álava, Pedro Jacinto de, 46, 48, 51–52, 59, 90
Álava province. *See also* Basque Country
    emigration and influence from, 1, 3, 17, 25
    RSBAP of, 48–50, 52, 54, 56
    women's education in, 71
Aldaco, Manuel de, 20, 23, 25, 76
Aldaco y Fagoaga, Juan José de, 25
Altuna, Manuel Ignacio de, 46
Alzate, José Antonio, 74
Las Amigas (The Friends), 9
Apartado, Marquis of, 19, 76
Aránzazu, Virgin of, 17, 74
Aránzazu Guild, 17–26, 29, 72–73, 75, 77
Arcos Herrera, Carol, 74
asset concentration policy, 2
Azlor y Echeverz, María Ignacia de, 12–14, 23, 44, 45, 72
Azlor y Virto de Vera, José de, 12, 13

Basque Country
    18th century education of women from (*see* Basque Country women's education; Basque-Mexican women's education)
    emigration to America from, 1–4, 8–9, 13–14, 16–25
    femininity in (*see* femininity)
    inheritance policies in, 2
    legal and geographic framework of, 1, 5n2 (*see also specific provinces*)
Basque Country women's education. *See also* Basque-Mexican women's education
    attendance in, 40
    beginnings of, 39–44, 71
    Bergara Soledad Seminary for, 41–52, 59–60, 71–72
    context for, 1–4
    costs of, 40
    evolution of, 71–81
    home education vs., 40, 74
    Munibe's (Peñaflorida's) influence on and goals for, 46–48, 50–54, 59–60, 71
    options for orientation of, 10, 40
    (*see also* marriage and motherhood; religious vows; spinsterhood)
    RSBAP and (*see Real Sociedad Bascongada de los Amigos del País*)
    Seminary for Young Ladies of Vitoria for, 54–56, 58–59, 71
    social hierarchy and, 40–41, 43, 48–50, 54–60, 72
Basque lobby, 2, 8–9
Basque-Mexican women's education
    Basque Country education and, 52, 71–81
    context for, 1–4
    emigration and influence on, 2, 8–9, 13–14, 16–25

evolution of Mexican women's education and, 9–16, 72
legal and geographic location for, 5n2
Mexican independence and, 16, 74–78, 81
RSBAP and, 20–22, 72–74, 81
scholarships for, 12, 19–20, 25
secular, 22–23, 26, 29, 52
social hierarchy and, 10, 13, 72, 74
Vizcaínas School for, 8, 16–29, 72–73, 75–78, 84*t*–87*t*, 89*t*
Bassoco, Antonio, 15, 75, 77
Bassoco, José María, 22
Bassoco family, 19
Belarmino, Cardinal, 11
Belem retreat, 9. *See also Colegio de Belem*
Bergara Patriotic Seminary. *See* Patriotic Bergara Seminary
Bergara Soledad Seminary, 41–52
beginnings of, 41–44, 71–72
constitution and purpose of, 42–43, 46–50
financing of, 44–48
location of, 50–51
opening of, 52, 71
RSBAP and, 42, 46–52, 59–60
Berroeta, Clara de, 41–42, 43
Bilbao
libraries in, 56
women's education in, 41–42

Cabañas, Juan Ruiz de, 76
Calatayud, Father, 43
Carlos III, 50, 71
Castañiza, Juan Francisco de, 16
Castañiza family, 19
Castorena y Ursúa, Ignacio de, 12
Catherine the Great, 54, 73
Colegio de Belem (Belem School), 10–12, 19–20, 23, 26, 28, 74, 77–78. *See also* Belem retreat
Colegio de la Madre de Dios (the School of the Mother of God), 9
Colegio de las Vizcaínas. See Vizcaínas School
El Colombiano, 76

Compañía de María (Company of Mary)
in Basque Country, 45–47, 50, 52–53, 59
gender role stance of, 79, 81
in Mexico, 11, 13–16, 29, 72–73
Convento de la Concepción (the Convent of the Conception), 9
Crisis of 1600, 4
La culta latiniparla (Quevedo), 11

*docta-hombruna (*learned-masculine woman), 53
Doctrina Cristiana (Belarmino), 11
dowries, 12, 59, 60, 90

Echeverz, Ignacia Xaviera de, 13
Echeveste, Francisco de, 15, 20, 23–25, 88*t*–89*t*
education, Basque women's. *See* Basque Country women's education; Basque-Mexican women's education
Education des filles (Fénelon), 11–12
Eguía, Joaquín de, 22
Eguiara y Eguren, Juan José de, 19
emigration, 1–4, 8–9, 13–14, 16–25
Enlightenment
Basque-Mexican women's education influenced by, 16, 20, 22, 72–74
Bergara Soledad Seminary influenced by, 44, 46–52
end of Basque, 71
gender conceptions in, 53, 56–57, 73–74, 79–81
Munibe (Gaspar de) as exponent of, 21
RSBAP as institution of, 20, 22, 42, 46–52, 54–57, 74, 76 (*see also Real Sociedad Bascongada de los Amigos del País*)
transatlantic influence of, 73–74
Erasmus of Rotterdam, 10

Fagoaga e Yragorri, Francisco de, 20
Fagoaga family, 19, 76
femininity, 4, 11–12, 52, 58, 73, 79–81
Fénelon, 11–12
Ferdinand VI, 21, 22–23

Fernández de Jáuregui, María, 11
Fernando VI, 15
Fernando VII, 78
Foncerrada, José Bernardo de, 76
foral system, 2
France, women's education in, 11, 27, 41, 48, 53
Francis Xavier, Saint, 9, 17

Gálvez, Bernardo de, 76
Gamboa, Francisco Xavier de, 16, 23, 76
Gárate, José de, 12
Goizueta Van Breuseghem, Magdalena de, 44, 45–46, 48, 51, 52, 59–60, 71–72
Goizueta y Echeverz, Juan Manuel de, 44–45
Gortázar family, 56, 72, 93*t*
Guadalupe, Virgin of, 74
Guardiola, Marquis of, 19, 76
Guevara, Catalina Vélez de, 41
Guipúzcoa province. *See also* Basque Country
  emigration and influence from, 1, 3, 17, 20, 25
  libraries in, 56
  men's education in, 21 (*see also* Patriotic Bergara Seminary)
  women's education in, 39–60, 71

home education, 9, 14, 27, 40, 74

Ignatius of Loyola, Saint, 13, 17, 51, 74, 77, 81
independence, Mexican, 16, 74–78, 81
inheritance policies, 2
Iraeta, Ana de, 77
Iturbide, Agustín de, 78
Iturbide, José Joaquín de, 76
Iturrigaray, Viceroy, 76

Lacunza, José María, 25
Lambert, Mme. de, 11
Lanciego y Eguilaz, José de, 9–10
Larramendi, Manuel de, 42–43
Leizaola y Lili, Manuel de, 42

León, Juan Francisco de, 44
León, Luis de, 10
Lestonnac, Jeanne de, 13
libraries, 41, 56, 92*t*–93*t*
literature, 57, 80
Loyola Sanctuary, 51
Luther, Martin, 10

Mariá Josefa, 94n1
Marian Patriots, 77–78
marriage and motherhood
  dowries for, 12, 59, 60, 90
  Enlightenment views of, 16, 27, 47, 56–57, 73, 79–81
  "republican mother" image for, 27, 73
  women's education in preparation for, 10, 12, 16, 28, 40–41, 47–50, 53, 55–58
Mazarredos family, 72
Meave, Ambrosio de, 20, 21–22, 23, 25
Mendizábal e Iraeta, Gabriel de, 75
Mexico
  Basque women's education in (*see* Basque-Mexican women's education)
  independence of, 16, 74–78, 81
Michael, Saint, 9
Los mil ángeles custodios de María Santísima girls' school, 12
Mina, Navarran Xavier, 76
Miranda, Agustín Juárez de, 94n1
Miranda, Francisco, 76
Mística Ciudad de Dios (Ágreda), 11
Modesto Ordoñana, Antonio, 15
Molière, 11
Montehermoso, Marchioness of, 41
Montehermoso, Marquis of. *See* Velasco, José María Aguirre Ortés de
motherhood. *See* marriage and motherhood
Mucientes, Francisco, 46
Munibe, Gaspar de (Count of Valdelirios), 21, 53
Munibe, Xavier María de (Count of Peñaflorida)
  Basque Country educational influence and goals of, 46, 47–48, 50–54, 59–60, 71

Basque-Mexican influence of, 20–21
death of, changes following, 71, 81
dowry system proposal by, 59, 60, 90
Munibe e Idiáquez, Alonso María de, 42
municipal Basque education. *See* Basque
  Country women's education
Muriel, Josefina, 12
music education, 12, 28, 43, 57

Napoleon, invasion by, 74–75
Narros, Marquis of, 46, 50
national brotherhoods, 84*t*
Navarra, Kingdom of. *See also* Basque Country
  emigration and influence from/to, 1,
    13–14, 17–19, 25
  libraries in, 56
  women's education in, 14, 39, 41, 48,
    53 (*see also* Basque Country women's
    education; Tudela *Enseñanza*)
Nieremberg, Eusebio de, 11
nobility
  privileged status of, 3 (*see also* social
    hierarchy)
  women's education founded in, 26
novels, 57
Nuestra Señora de Aránzazu (Our Lady of
  Aránzazu) Guild, 18
*Nuestra Señora de Guadalupe y San Luis
  Gonzaga* Convent, 16
Nuestra Señora de la Enseñanza (Our Lady
  of Teaching), 45
Nuestra Señora del Pilar Convent, 14

Ocampo, Melchor, 25
Olaso y Zumalabe, Miguel José de, 43, 46, 50
Olavide, Pablo de, 48–50, 51, 52, 54, 58, 73, 79
Ortiz, Josefa, 78
Oyarzabal, Luis de, 25

Patriotic Bergara Seminary, 21–22, 50–51,
  54, 59
Pazuegos, Bernardo, 14
Peñaflorida, Count of. *See* Munibe, Xavier
  María de
Peru, Basque emigration to, 2

Les Précieuses ridicules (Molière), 11
primogeniture system, 2

Quevedo, Francisco de, 11

*Real Colegio de Nuestra Señora de Gudalupe
  de Indias* (Royal School of Our Lady of
  Guadalupe of the Indies), 15–16
Real Colegio de San Ignacio de México (Royal
  School of Saint Ignatius Mexico). *See
  Vizcaínas* School
Real Compañía Guipuzcoana de Caracas
  (RCGC), 44–45, 46
*Real Sociedad Bascongada de los Amigos del
  País* (RSBAP, or the Royal Basque
  Society of Friends of the Country),
  20–22, 42, 46–60, 72–78, 81
religious vows, 10, 40, 49, 59
Los Remedios, Virgin of, 78
Rocaverde, Marquis of, 42, 50
Rubio y Salinas, Manuel, 12, 23
Russia, women's education in, 54, 73

Salcedo y Chávarri, María Antonia de, 41
salons, women's learning in, 57
Samaniego y Munibe, Félix Maria Ignacio
  Sánchez de, 46, 49, 53, 54, 72, 80
San Ignacio Guild, 17–23
San Luis Gonzaga Schools, 28
San Miguel and San Francisco Xavier retreat,
  9. *See also Colegio de Belem*
San Miguel de Aguayo, Marquis of, 12, 13,
  19, 75, 76
Santa Clara Convent/Seminary, 41, 53
scholarships, 12, 19–20, 25
Seminary (or House of Education) for
  Young Ladies of Vitoria, 54–56, 58–59,
  71
silver trade, 2, 20, 24
Smolnyi Institute, 54
social hierarchy
  in Basque Country women's education,
    40–41, 43, 48–50, 54–60, 72
  in Basque-Mexican women's
    education, 10, 13, 72, 74

Mexican independence and, 76, 77–78
privileged status of nobility and, 3
Society of Jesus, 13–14, 29, 46, 50, 52, 75–77, 79, 81
Society of Mary, 23
Soroa, Ana María de, 41
Spain, Kingdom of
    Basque emigration and influence in colonial empire of, 1–4, 8–9, 13–14, 16–25
    Mexican independence from, 16, 74–78, 81
    Napoleon's invasion of, Mexican support for Spain against, 74–75
    national brotherhoods in, 84*t*
Spanish language, education in, 43, 54
spinsterhood, 10, 40, 59–60

Tagle, Luis Sánchez de, 24
teachers
    in Basque Country education, 39–40, 47, 49–50, 55
    in Mexico, 9, 13, 22, 28
    women educated to be, 16
Lo temporal y Eterno (Nieremberg), 11
Torres, Juan de, 24
Tudela *Enseñanza*, 14, 41–42, 45–48, 50, 53–54, 59, 72

United States, women's education in, 27–28, 73
Urbina family, 56, 60, 72, 91*t*–92*t*
Uribe, Francisco Fernández de, 12

Valdelirios, Count of. *See* Munibe, Gaspar de
Velasco, José María Aguirre Ortés de, 53–54, 57–58, 79
Vicario, María Leona, 78

Vitoria
    libraries in, 56
    Seminary for Young Ladies of, 54–56, 58–59, 71
Vives, Juan Luis, 10
Vizarrón y Eguiarreta, Juan Antonio de, 12, 19, 74
Vizcaínas School (Vizcayan Girls' School)
    cost and funding of, 20, 23, 24, 72, 84*t*–87*t*
    emigration and influence on, 8–9, 13–14, 16–25
    evolution of women's education in Mexico prior to, 9–16
    founding and origins of, 8, 16–25, 72–73
    life at, 26–29
    loans granted by, 89*t*
    Mexican independence and, 75–76, 77–78
    purpose of, 26
    scholarships for, 19–20, 25
    secular jurisdiction for, 22–23, 26, 29
    student population of, 26, 28–29, 72, 77
Vizcaya, Lordship of. *See also* Basque Country
    education of girls from, in Mexico, 8, 16–29 (*see also Vizcaínas* School)
    emigration and influence from, 1, 3, 17, 20, 25
    RSBAP of, 48, 55
    women's education in, 71

Wollstonecraft, Mary, 56
women's education, Basque 18th century. *See* Basque Country women's education; Basque-Mexican women's education

Zumárraga, Juan de, 9, 16

www.ingramcontent.com/pod-product-compliance
Lightning Source LLC
Chambersburg PA
CBHW070734230426
43665CB00016B/2241